NOSTRADAMUS
The Secret Revelations

NOSTRADAMUS
The Secret Revelations

ALLAN HALL

INDEX

© Orbis Publishing 1996

This edition first published in Great Britain in 1996 specially for
Index
Unit 1
Garrard Way
Kettering NN16 8TD

ISBN-1 900 761 11 4

Printed and bound in Italy

Contents

Introduction

Ever since he first published his amazing series of quatrains more than 400 years ago, Nostradamus has fascinated and beguiled generations with his seemingly uncanny ability to predict the future. Incredibly, he seems to have seen the major events and upheavals of each century, carefully disguising them in his often enigmatic quatrains.

But as each successive generation comes to study and understand the works of this greatest of all seers, new revelations have been discovered buried within the puns, anagrams and code words he used in order to avoid the witch-hunters of 16th century France. Some of his most memorable prophecies can only be understood in hindsight – for instance, his classic forecast concerning man's landing on the moon in 1969 was a total riddle before that famous July day – but many do allow interpretation to take place in advance of events.

Of course, that opens the scholar to error, even ridicule. Today, some of the most prominent Nostradamus interpreters are being maligned for their perceived outlandish assessments of his works. Yet without their efforts, every one of his quatrains would be subject to interpretation after the event. And where is the mystery – even fun – in that?

No, when Nostradamus sat down in his tiny study all those centuries ago, he wanted those who followed him to uncover the secrets of his quatrains in the hope that man could somehow avert the dire future and events that awaited him. Indeed, Nostradamus always insisted that his predictions were not set in stone – and that they could be averted if man heeded his warning signs and acted accordingly to change his ways.

In this book, we have sought to offer the latest interpretations of his works. Many of those quatrains analysed herein are of events and things not yet come to pass, which means, of course, that no one can be certain of their accuracy. But Nostradamus always left clues within his quatrains as to their exact meanings. And that is all one can go on – with the help of guidelines set by trends unfolding in the world today.

That, of course, is one of the great marvels of Nostradamus. As we noted earlier, his quatrains speak to all generations. But it is our generation, on the cusp of the millennium, that he seems to be reaching out to across the grey mists of time. Nostradamus was worried – yet at times hopeful – about the age in which we live. Why? Why us, of all those who have come before and those likely to come after? Maybe it is because for the first time in our history, we have the technology to end the world. With nuclear bombs we can turn it into a lifeless, smouldering heap of rubble many times over; we can wipe out entire nations with chemical or biological weapons; the modern plague of AIDS, which targets our very life cycle, is a threat hovering over us all; terrorism fights to light the fuse of a new holocaust; and our careless disregard for the environment threatens our ozone layer, our rivers, our streams – even the very air we breathe.

It is in light of all these threats to our existence that Nostradamus's predictions cry out for new interpretations. What does he see lying in wait for those of us who live in this very decade? Is there a way out of all the turmoil? New insights suggest there are terrible events about to unfold within the lifetimes of most of the readers of this book. Plagues, great natural disasters, nuclear exchanges, heightened terrorism and a general malaise which he believed will threaten every single inhabitant of this planet.

With these multiple swords of Damocles hanging precariously over our heads, dare we revisit the works of the man who saw it all? We cannot simply stand by while these modern-day scourges ravish the planet – so why not look for answers, indeed help, in his quatrains? That is the challenge to this generation of Nostradamus scholars: to reinterpret, to find new meaning in his Centuries, to follow the unexplored 'sign posts' he left for us within his writings.

But while the emphasis of this book is on the new, one cannot properly study – or appreciate – Nostradamus without looking back on those quatrains which have already come to pass. Why? Because by its very nature, the late 20th century is a cynical age. We believe little we cannot touch, see, smell or hear. So by revisiting some of his earlier predictions – and seeing their amazingly accurate details with the kind hindsight of history – the reader will begin to better appreciate why some people believe Nostradamus was the genuine article, a man who really could see through time.

But even some of the quatrains thought to have referred to times long since gone can be open to reinterpretation. For instance, as the reader will come to see, some of his riddles about World War I and other massive upheavals have only recently been given new assessments that are said to hold incredible warnings for both our generation and the one immediately to follow.

That is why Nostradamus's works are constantly being revisited by scholars today. They are looking for the new meaning, the new warning, the new revelation.

In this book, we will look at the very latest interpretations of many of his vast writings. But be warned. There is evil lurking in our time, and the great prophet of Salon saw it clearly. Now, armed with these new insights into his quatrains, we can change our course if only we are ready to follow him.

It is up to all of us to listen to the warnings he set down for us.

CHAPTER ONE

Nostradamus: His life and times

A man of strange and brilliant talents

◆

How did Nostradamus become aware of his amazing powers? Did he have a sudden revelation, or was it a gradual awakening to the fact that he was no ordinary man? Relatively little is known about his early days, leaving even his life story open to new discoveries and interpretations.

One of the greatest riddles about the man himself - the process by which he came to experience his marvellous visions - has never been fully explained. Did he go into a trance, use water divination or stare into a simmering pot of bizarre concoctions? Indeed, all these centuries after his death, there is still some dispute among scholars about his precise methods of prophecy. In this chapter, we look at the most up-to-date research.

Did he actually hear the future, as well as see it? Again, new analysis holds the key to the mystery. In this chapter, we will examine the latest insights into those enigmas and learn more about how and why it came to pass that this man should be so blessed with such strange powers.

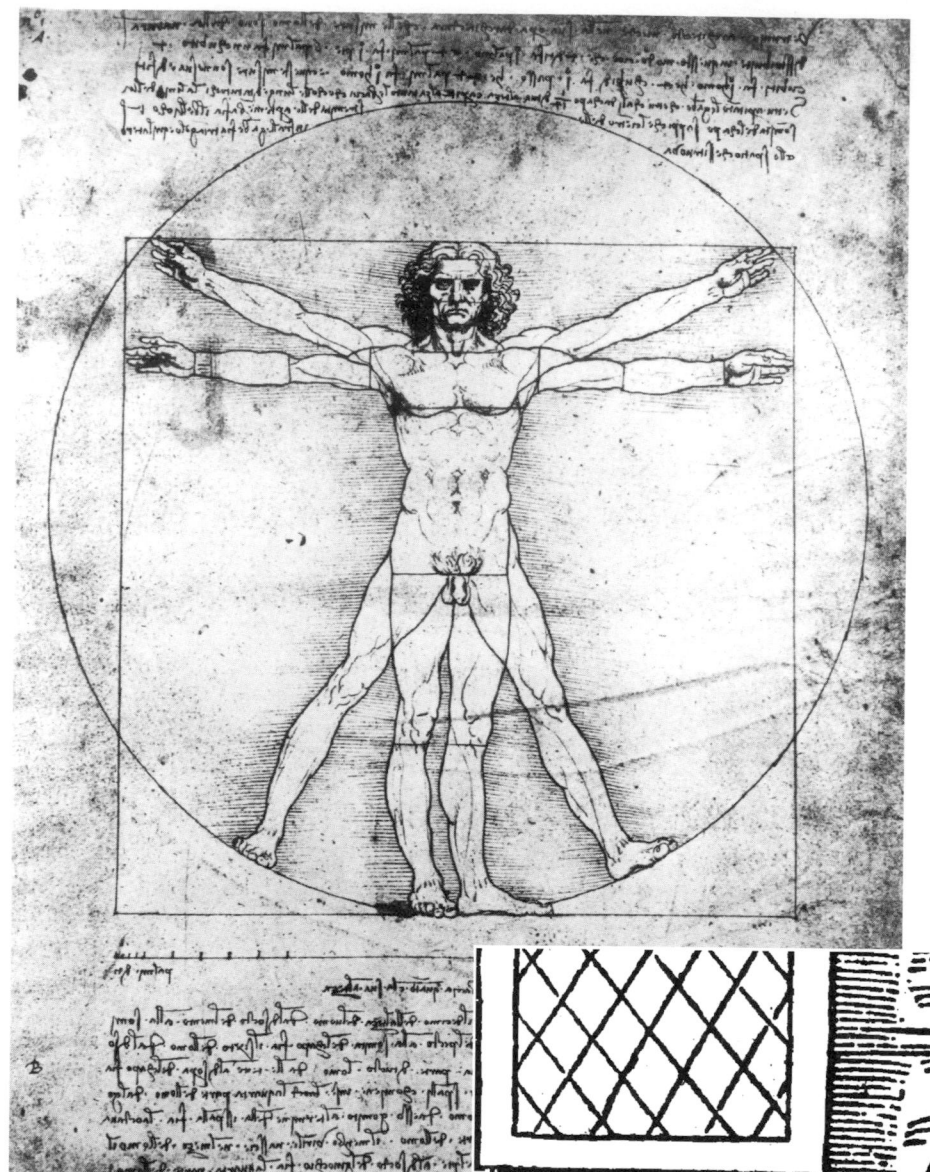

was finally awakening from the long night of the Dark Ages that had descended upon the continent a thousand years before, when the Roman Empire fell before the onslaught of the barbarian tribes from the north.

Light in the Darkness

As the 16th century dawned, there was a renewed sense of learning in all disciplines of science and the arts, particularly in Italy and France, home to some of the most creative and fertile minds of the age. Great universities were dedicated, young students were tutored in mathematics, astronomy, medicine and history, and the genius of men like Leonardo da Vinci, Michelangelo and Thomas More flowered without hindrance. However, it was not all light

Left: The great Renaissance, typified by the scientific and artistic genius of Leonardo da Vinci, was in full flower when Nostradamus was born.

Below: However, the same century also saw acts of extraordinary savagery and evil, such as the widespread persecution of supposed witches.

History is scattered with the names of a few gifted individuals with the power to see into the future. The Irish monk, St. Malachy, envisioned the reigns of popes who would lead the Catholic Church throughout the centuries; the legendary Mother Shipton, born in the reign of Henry VII, saw astonishingly accurate visions of motorized transport and weird flying machines; Cheiro predicted the death of kings with unnerving certainty. None of these, though, could equal the brilliance of Michel de Nostradame – or Nostradamus as he is now better known.

The great prophet was born in the small French town of St-Rémy, Provence, on 14 December 1503. It was the time of the Renaissance, and Europe

and learning. This was also the time of the Inquisition, of great upheaval, plague and war. Innocents were tortured and killed as sorcerers or witches, Martin Luther was leading a revolution of ideas against the Roman Church, and great armies slaughtered each other on battlefields from Sicily to Scotland.

It was into this world of grandeur and horror, of learning and superstition, that Nostradamus was born, the first son of Jacques and Renée de Nostradame, who were themselves both children of widely-respected doctors. It has been said in some quarters that Michel's forefathers were Jewish, and that they converted to Christianity to escape the terrible iniquities inflicted upon Jews throughout the Middle Ages and beyond. However,

while scholars debate his religious ancestry, there is no doubt he remained a fervent supporter of the Papacy throughout his life.

Jacques de Nostradame was a notary public. He was a kind, decent man, who encouraged the young boy along the path of learning and helped instruct him in the ways of the church. However, it was Michel's two grandfathers, Jean de St-Rémy and Pierre Nostradame, who shaped much of what he would become. They helped school him in all the required disciplines of the time, including Latin, natural laws, maths and astronomy. Michel was an eager pupil. Many nights, he would sit in fascination at the feet of the two elderly scholars, his eyes ablaze with the wonders they taught

Above: When Nostradamus was growing up, the scientific orthodoxy was that the Earth was the centre of the Universe. Nostradamus challenged this view when he was still a young student.

him. So much so that by the age of 13, he had knowledge of the sciences far beyond his years, and had gained a reputation in the town as a boy genius.

Written in the Stars

His maternal grandfather also tutored the boy in astrology and fortune telling, which were widely accepted disciplines at the time. Indeed, most royal courts of Europe had official astrologers, who were courted and admired by the aristocrats of the day. Michel was an avid pupil, and voraciously read whatever books were available on the

was just 16. There, he studied for his Philosophia, the 16th-century equivalent of a Bachelor of Arts degree. It was during this time that Michel's promise really began to bloom, and he amazed his teachers and fellow students with his intelligence, knowledge and incredible powers of memory. In fact, it has been said that Michel would only need to read anything once in order to instantly commit it to memory.

Astonishingly, he also insisted to those who would listen that the Earth revolved around the Sun – an idea that would land the Polish astronomer Nicolaus Copernicus in more than a little trouble several years later!

Hero of the Plague

As brilliant as he was, Michel was never boastful or vain. Indeed, reports of the time paint him as a modest, unassuming young man, only too eager to help others with their lessons. After completing his studies in Avignon, Michel returned home to St-Rémy, where he and his parents discussed what profession he would take up. Michel really wanted to study astronomy, but his father is said to have persuaded him to follow instead in

Left and below: Astrology, the art of divination using the stars as a guide, was a respected scientific pursuit in the 16th century. Young Michel learned it from his maternal grandfather.

mystical arts. His grandfathers, both widely-travelled men, had built up impressive libraries and collected works both modern and ancient from all corners of the continent and beyond. It's known that Jean de St-Rémy had what we might today call psychic powers, though his proficiency in them is not known. Certainly, his talents never equalled those of the rosy-cheeked lad he instructed.

Michel's parents decided to send him to Avignon, site of one of the great universities in all of France, when he

REVOLUTIONARY THEORIES

Nicolaus Copernicus was born in 1473 in Thorn, on the banks of the Vistula River in northern Poland. An orphan by the age of 10, he was taken by his uncle, who later became a bishop, to the city of Frauenburg where he was raised and later appointed canon. He showed an early skill in the science of mathematics, and was a life-long devotee to astronomy, which he pursued as an amateur.

His publication of *De revolutionibus orbium coelestium* – which asserted that the Earth and the other planets revolved around a stationary Sun – caused much heated debate at the time. Copernicus was vilified by contemporary religious leaders such as Martin Luther and John Calvin. Luther referred to him as "an upstart astrologer", declaring that "This fool wishes to reverse the entire science of astronomy." Surprisingly, the Catholic Church took a far more tolerant view of Copernicus's theory, which eventually began to be taught in Catholic universities.

Top right: Nostradamus was a pupil, and later a teacher, at the famous Faculté du Médecin in Montpellier.

Right: Copernicus's On the Revolution of Heavenly Bodies, published in 1543, set out a new model of the Universe.

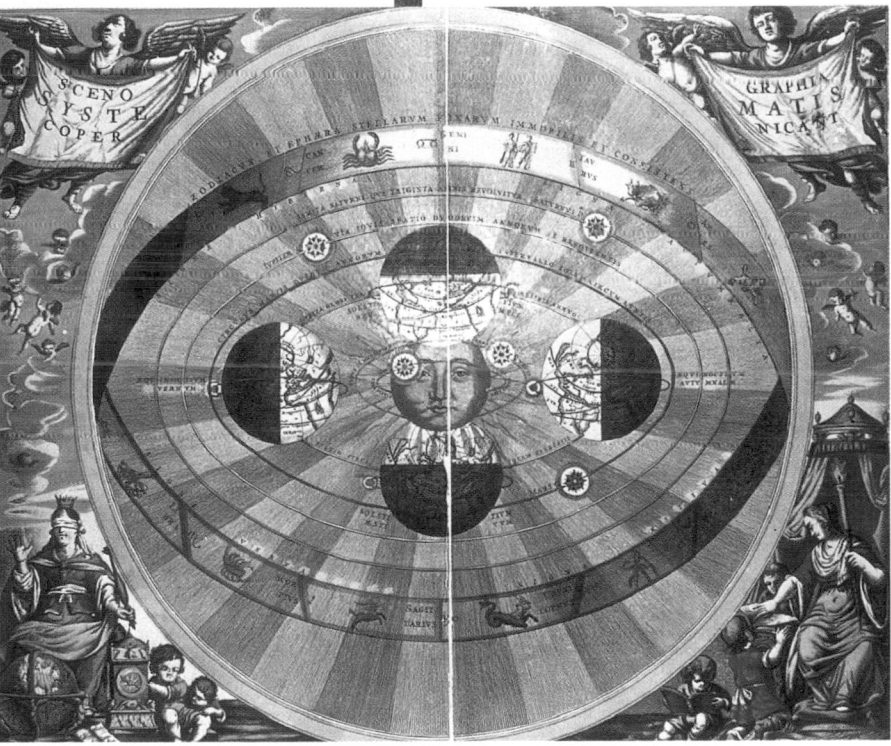

cure the sick, so he took to the countryside, where villagers and farm workers gratefully accepted any help they were offered – even if it was from a young, inexperienced student.

Michel soon proved he was a far greater healer than any other doctor of his day. In fact, if Nostradamus had not made a single prophecy in his entire life, he would still be remembered and hailed today as a medical genius, worthy of all of history's accolades.

He wandered from town to town, and the plague retreated before him. His fame slowly spread from Carcassonne to Bordeaux as he single-handedly cured the sick and dying. For four years, he patiently and quietly attacked the killer disease head on, and people clamoured for his services. Everywhere he went, great crowds came out to greet him, often throwing rose petals in his path as he entered their cities, like a conquering

the illustrious footsteps of his grandfathers and become a doctor.

So he went to the Faculté de Médecin in Montpellier, then the most acclaimed university for scientific study in the country. However, Michel's stay there was short. When he was 21, a great plague descended upon Europe, laying waste to cities and villages throughout the continent, and the university, like many institutions of the day, was forced to close its doors.

Unlike the other students, who fled to their home towns in a bid to escape the

horrors of the plague, Michel decided to join the fight against it, though he shunned the widely-used methods such as 'bleeding' – removing impure blood from the system by opening a vein or attaching leeches. He realized that a medical student, who had no right to practise medicine, could not just barge into a local hospital and start trying to

hero of old. Soon, he was known throughout France – and he was not yet 26 years old.

Just how he fought the plague is not known. Many scholars believe it might have been a mixture of exotic potions and compounds derived from Arabic ideas of medicine. His grandfathers had a knowledge of such things, so he may have

DEATH STALKS THE LAND

No-one is certain exactly what disease it was that plagued France in the 1520s. Some think it may have been the black plague, so named because it left its victims looking like they had been charred by fire. Others believe it might have been the mysterious 'sweating sickness' that ravaged parts of England a few years later.

No matter what it was, it had a devastating effect, particularly in southern France. People died in such vast numbers – and so rapidly – that piles of bodies lay where they fell, on the city streets and rural highways alike. Doctors had no answers to it, and whatever solutions they did try had no effect in stemming the tide of death.

At least many of them tried to help, even though they put themselves at great risk by doing so. To protect themselves, they wore extra clothing and plugged their noses with cotton, because it had been discovered that the plague travelled through the air or by touch. They also took to wearing goggles to protect their eyes, and smeared their clothing in garlic oil, known from ancient Greek times to be a purifying agent.

had access to ancient prescriptions which Eastern physicians had long used to combat the scourge of plague in their own lands. He probably found the ingredients he needed in the woods and fields among the herbs and flowers, because whatever the cure was, it was needed in great quantities and he certainly did not have the money or time to brew up elaborate concoctions. One claim, often repeated down through the years, is that he used a mixture of gold and lapis lazuli, but this is patently absurd. After all, how would a young medical student obtain such expensive minerals?

The terrifying plague defeated, the young hero returned at last to his medical studies at Montpellier, where he sat for his final exams having being credited with the four years he spent curing the incurable. He passed without a problem, and was invited by the

faculty to stay on at the university as a teacher. He declined at first, preferring to travel and learn, but was eventually persuaded to stay after the students demanded he be their tutor!

Years of Wandering

His restless spirit would not allow him to stay in one place for long, though, and he soon informed his fellow teachers that he was leaving the university. They reluctantly accepted his decision, and bade farewell to their most prized and famous member. For the next few years, he travelled throughout the south of France, where he was always warmly greeted by townsfolk as the man who had extinguished the plague.

He was a much sought-after physician, who catered to the wealthy as well as the poor, and his pockets were lined with enough gold to allow him to

Above: In the 16th century, a peasant's life was one of of unremitting toil. With no money for medicine, they relied on the help of men such as Nostradamus.
Left: Epidemic plagues were the scourge of medieval Europe. Ailments such as the mysterious Black Death destroyed rich and poor alike.
Below: Those who could afford to pay for medical help were not much better off: physicians had no answer to the plague save for practices like blood-letting.

work as he pleased. During this time he settled in Agen, where he met and married a young woman whose name has since been lost. We only know that she was 'very lovely and very lovable', to quote records of the time.

They had two sons, and the years spent in Agen were among the happiest of the great man's life. Fate, however, would soon intervene in the form of another plague, which took his entire

Above: In his own time – this painting was made from a sketch taken in life – Nostradamus's reputation was based as much on his medical skills as it was on his remarkable prophecies.

family from him. Nostradamus was inconsolable at the loss of his wife and two beloved children. He had saved thousands from this dreadful death, but could not even save his own family. New research shows that Nostradamus's standing as a doctor took a severe nose-dive after his family's demise. After all, argued his critics, if he were such a brilliant man, why couldn't he save his

own loved ones? Even his wife's family turned against him, suing him for the return of her dowry.

More frighteningly, detractors came out of the woodwork to denounce him as a dangerous heretic. Recently-uncovered evidence reveals that, some years earlier, he had made an off-the-cuff remark to a worker casting a bronze statue of the Virgin Mary. He joked that the man was casting demons. Nostradamus meant it as a good-humoured reference to the man's less than perfect workmanship, but now that his previously unassailable reputation was under attack, the workman came forward to tell the story to Church officials, who demanded the doctor answer to a charge of heresy. He was ordered to be brought before a tribunal of inquisitors at Toulouse, where he knew he might be put to the torture. Nostradamus fled before he could be called to appear.

Heartbroken, he decided to return to the life that had once suited him so well. At the age of 30, he took once more to the roads and byways of the countryside, and spent the next 10 years travelling, gathering new medicines and knowledge of life as he wandered through France and Italy, where he stayed for a time in Milan, Genoa and Venice. Even though

little is known of his life during this long period of wandering and learning, scholars have no doubt that this is when he first began to have his incredible visions of things to come.

Settling in Salon

In 1543, Nostradamus, who was nearing 40, decided to settle down once more, and selected the town of Salon, which was centrally placed to the main cities in Provence. Despite his years of travel and the wonders he had seen, the doctor still preferred the peace and tranquillity of small-town life to the bustle of the big cities.

After settling down in Salon, he began to think of writing down his visions. Of course, it was not so simple an idea. The period was rife with religious intolerance, and torture awaited those caught dabbling in the 'black arts'. However, Nostradamus was a fervent believer in the Almighty, and thought his visions were the work of God, not the Devil. In fact, he may have begun writing his *Centuries* – in which the verses known as quatrains were compiled – inside a long-forgotten

Below: The tribunals of the Inquisition, designed to root out heretics and unbelievers from the Catholic Church, were greatly feared; Nostradamus fled rather than face one.

monastery, protected by good men of faith who knew this gentle healer was no slave to Satan.

Nostradamus always believed his power was inherited, probably from his maternal grandfather, and was God-given. "Through some eternal power," he once explained, "and epileptic Herculean excitement, celestial causation is made known to me ... but the perfect knowledge of causes cannot be acquired without divine inspiration. All authentic prophecy derives its first principle from God the Creator, next from favouring conditions, and last from natural endowment."

He married his second wife, Anne Ponsart Jumelle, a wealthy and beautiful

Above: Plague hospitals like this were little more than way-stations for the dying, although a few gifted physicians such as Nostradamus managed to bring real hope where none existed.

widow, and settled down to a comfortable life practising his medicine and contemplating the visions he was seeing. Soon, they were blessed with a son, whom he named César. But once again, as it so often did, fate dragged Nostradamus away from the carefree existence of a country doctor. He heard, through a passing traveller, that plague had again broken out in Aix, the capital of Provence. Eventually, the city fathers called him in to help the sick, but not before a sizeable proportion of the population had succumbed.

Renewed Fame

Nostradamus, as usual not fearing for his own safety, heeded the call for help. For the next nine months, he threw himself into the fight as the body count continued to rise all around him. Eventually, just as he had been more than a decade earlier, he was victorious. The plague subsided, and all of France once again began to hail this worker of miracles. Soon, tiny Salon was inundated by the members of the nobility, who poured in to consult with him.

Left: The verdicts of the tribunals of the Inquisition were publicly announced at an auto-da-fé, where sentences such as death by burning were carried out immediately.

THE GIFT OF PROPHECY

During his time in Italy, Nostradamus had one of his first recorded glimpses into the future. He was walking down a narrow street, when he passed a group of Franciscan friars leading a herd of swine. With them was a young boy who had only recently joined the order. As Nostradamus neared the lad, he dismounted from his mule, walked up to him and immediately went down on one knee. When the startled friars asked him why he would bow down and show obeisance to one so young, Nostradamus replied that he must kneel before 'His Holiness'.

Astonishingly, years after the death of the prophet, that simple country boy, Felice Peretti, became Pope Sixtus V. It's also interesting to note that Nostradamus was no fan of the future pope he met that day. In fact, his later forecast that the cardinals would "Elect one who comes from the country, and wears the black and grey robe" came with the warning that "Never was there one more sly." Obviously, the deeply religious Nostradamus was paying homage to the office of the Papacy when he bowed to young Peretti, and not to the man himself.

During his decade of wandering, Nostradamus gave another famous display of his amazing powers. In Lorraine, he was invited to a feast at a castle owned by a friend, Lord Florinville. Florinville, sceptical of the doctor's growing reputation for psychic abilities, decided to put him to the test. As they walked through the courtyard, they spotted two pigs, one black, the other white. His friend casually asked Nostradamus to predict the fate of the two animals. The seer told him the white one would be taken by a wolf, and that the black one would be served at dinner that night.

It was then that Florinville decided to play a trick, and instructed his cook to prepare the white pig for dinner. That night, as the guests sat down at the large ornate table, the host, with great glee, told Nostradamus he was eating the white pig. The doctor disagreed, insisting it was the black one, as he had forecast. Florinville summoned the cook to settle the argument. He was stunned to hear her tale. After she had cooked the white pig, she confessed, a tame wolf cub who was quartered at the castle walked into her kitchen and made a meal of it. She had no choice but to kill the black one and prepare it. Lord Florinville was convinced!

On another occasion, Nostradamus was said to have been lying in bed when a noisy ruckus broke out on the streets below. Suddenly, there was a sharp rap at the door and a young man came in. Nostradamus immediately recognized him as a page for a wealthy local family, and knew, without being told, that the family had lost one of its beloved dogs. Before the messenger could even stutter out the reason for his visit, the great prophet told him, with a dismissive wave of the hand, "You are making a lot of noise over a lost dog. Go and look on the road to Orléans. You will find it there on a leash." The stunned page sped off to the place where Nostradamus had 'seen' the missing pooch, and to his amazement found another servant on the road leading the dog back to the family's residence! However, Nostradamus's clairvoyant powers were usually put to more profound use.

Above: This French woodcut of Nostradamus in his study suggests he used astrology to make his predictions, but the truth is more complex than this.

Right: Omens and portents, including such natural wonders as comets, earthlights and animal behaviour, were used by lesser men than Nostradamus to predict the future.

Above: There is evidence that Nostradamus dabbled in alchemy. The often explosive quest to turn base metals into gold may have been a metaphor for the purification of the spirit.

His fellow physicians, though, were not so awe-struck. Driven by jealousy of his reputation and standing, they accused him of being in league with dark forces who, they claimed, had given him secret knowledge in return for his allegiance to Satan. However, not even their ridiculous accusations could affect his good name with the majority of his countrymen, and soon he was free once again to devote his energies to recording his amazing visions.

He converted the top floor of his home into a study and laboratory, where he would retreat every night once his children – there would be six of them – were sound asleep, and the daily duties of being a country doctor were complete.

He would spend hours at a time up there, seated at the long table where he kept an array of books and manuscripts, his writing equipment, a number of hourglasses, chemicals and some brass pots and urns. He became so wrapped up in his work that he often slept on a small bed in the corner. But Nostradamus, like many great men, needed little sleep, no more than five hours a night. In another corner was a tripod of solid brass, on which he sat. This was rumoured to have come from the famous Greek oracle at Delphi.

Some said he went into a trance whenever he saw his visions, while others believe he may have looked in a 'magic' mirror that hung on his wall. In the opening lines of the *Centuries*, Nostradamus himself explained that the ancient art of water divination played a role in his visions.

*"Seated at night in secret study,
Alone, at ease upon my tripod of brass.
From out of the low flame of solitude
Comes realization of that in which it is not
empty to believe."*

Century 1 Quatrain 1

*"Holding the bough with my hand where the
branches fork,
The Branch seeking the Ripple moistens the
hem of my robe and my foot,
Fear and a voice make me tremble in
my sleeves.
Splendour divine, the Divine Being is
seated near."*

Century I Quatrain 2

No-one is certain how it all took place, but the great man not only saw the future, he heard it as well. In quatrains revealing the horrors of World War II, for example, he clearly refers to the noise of strange flying machines. He not only heard the sounds of planes and bombs, but also the terrifying staccato clatter of machine-gun fire, as well, recent research has revealed, as the whine of the Soviet pipe rockets that demolished Berlin at the end of war.

Divine Inspiration

Still, the exact nature of the process by which he saw his – and our – future will never be known for sure. In another letter to César, he leaves no doubt that only the power of God could deliver such visions to him, through what he called illumination. "Though everlasting God alone knows His eternity of light, yet I speak frankly to all whose long, melancholy inspiration is transformed by the revelation of His immeasurable greatness. It is through the hidden source of divine light, manifested in two principal ways, that the understanding of the prophet is inspired. One way is the intuition which clarifies vision in him who predicts by the stars. The other is the prophecy by inspired revelation, which is practically a participation in divine eternity. In the latter, the prophet's judgment is according to his share of divine spirit which he has received through attunement with God the Creator, and also according to native endowment. The complete efficacy of illumination and the thin flame is to

WORDS OF POWER

In a letter to César, his eldest child, Nostradamus revealed something of the ancient books and manuscripts which helped him understand water divination. He also revealed his fears that he would be looked upon as a sorcerer because of that knowledge. "Although many volumes have come before me which have lain hidden for long ages, dreading what might happen in the future, after reading them, I made an offering of them to Vulcan," he said. "As the flame caught them, the fire, licking the air, flared in unaccustomed brightness, clearer than natural flame, more like the explosion of powder. It cast a subtle illumination over the house, as if it were filled by the reflection of the conflagration. So that you might not at some time be harmed by alchemic research for the perfect lunar or solar transformation, or the hidden, incorruptible metals of earth or sea, I reduced these books to ashes."

Scholars have long been fascinated by the origins of the ancient books that Nostradamus claimed to have used for his visions. It's quite likely he inherited them from his maternal grandfather, as Oriental books on magic were relatively easy to come by in Europe in the 15th century. It could also be that Nostradamus himself collected the books during his travels.

Researchers believe that the manuscript that dealt with water divination would most likely have come from ancient Greece, but as author Lee McCann points out in *Nostradamus: The Man Who Could See Through Time*, the great prophet did not rely on water divination alone to see his visions. "Nostradamus says more than once that his prophetic faculty was inherited. This ancient method of vision by water could have been stimulated, perhaps developed his gift to greater scope, but it never could have conferred it."

"That is why I have withheld my tongue from the vulgar and my pen from paper," he explained, "but later on, I thought I would, for the common good, describe the most important of the revolutionary changes I foresee, but so as not to upset my present readers I would do this in a clouded manner, with abstruse and twisted sentences, rather than being plainly prophetical."

His solution was to conceal his prophecies in riddles and cyphers. He wrote them in the form of four-line verses – quatrains. A hundred of these would make up a century, and he planned to complete twelve of these, though he eventually published just ten. To make it even harder for his enemies to accuse him of witchcraft, he further disguised his predictions by writing them in a hodgepodge of French, Latin, Greek, Hebrew, Italian and Provençal dialect. He also riddled them with symbolism and altered their time sequence to cause

recognize that what is predicted is true and of heavenly origin. For this light of prophecy descends from above no less than the light of day."

Nostradamus did not consider himself a prophet in the Biblical sense, as he made clear in the introduction to the prophecies. Rather, he says he is "the greatest sinner in the world, and heir to every human affliction, but, by being surprised sometimes by a prophetical mood, amid prolonged calculation, while engaged in nocturnal studies of sweet odour, I have composed books of prophecies, containing each one a hundred quatrains which I have joined obscurely and are perpetual vaticinations from now to the year 3797."

Although Nostradamus said his predictions would reach through to the year 3797 with the end of the Earth, once-secret revelations now disclose that they actually extend far beyond that time. For decades, many of his most puzzling quatrains could not be interpreted, but today, at the dawn of the Space Age, we have come to understand that the great prophet saw the future of mankind stretching beyond the hisory of the planet. It is, in the words of one modern scholar, "Proof that man will one day leave the bounds of Earth and settle in space."

Enigmatic Writings

Nostradamus had been keeping extensive records of his amazing visions for some time before he gradually came to believe that they should become known to others, so that they might come to see what lay ahead for man through him. He was well aware that he would have to be extremely careful in how he presented them to others, lest he be condemned as a witch. Close friends, such as the scholar and theologian Aymé de Chavigny, were privy to his astounding forecasts and agreed he should have them published, but they, too, saw the dangers inherent in presenting such grave predictions to an often foolish and generally highly superstitious audience.

Above: This 15th-century French tarot card of trump 18, The Moon, shows mediaeval astronomers – or perhaps astrologers – at work. Astrology predates astronomy as a science.

Above: This Renaissance ceiling shows the constellations. Those that make up the signs of the zodiac are named for their characters, not the pattern of the stars.

further confusion. One suggestion is that he tossed all his papers in the air, then assembled them in the order they fell. It certainly seems that way at times.

In his book, *They Saw Tomorrow*, Charles Neilson Gattey explains how difficult to understand Nostradamus made his quatrains: "Even today, when one first reads the original French edition, one's initial reaction is of perplexed disillusion. The language is enigmatic, at times almost unintelligible, as if written in code. The verses are not in chronological order, and jump about in time and subject. Strange sobriquets of Nostradamus's own coining are used for famous personalities. Everywhere we find mystifying puns and anagrams."

Ever since their publication, though, the quatrains have withstood the critics and doubters, and proved that Nostradamus was without equal in parting the veils of time. In 1555, he published the first volume of his *Centuries*. The middle of the 16th century was a heyday of astrology and prophecy,

and his fame spread like wildfire throughout Europe, even among the great masses who could neither read nor afford such luxury items as books. His renown transcended all social borders, as word-of-mouth told and retold his amazing visions, but it was among the highest levels of French society that his prophecies aroused the most interest.

Catherine des Médicis, queen consort of King Henri II, became an avid fan of the country doctor almost immediately. Catherine, a longtime devotee of astrology and occultism, even persuaded her husband to invite Nostradamus to Paris. This was an astonishing compliment. Although the capital was brimming with seers and astrologers of varying skills, a public invitation from royalty was unheard of. So, on 14 July 1555, Nostradamus – who was suffering from gout and no longer in good health – set out on the long, arduous road to Paris for his audience with the King.

It took Nostradamus four weeks to make the trip to Paris, and he arrived at journey's end tired and a little out of sorts. Upon his arrival, though, he was greeted with such warmth and acclaim that he soon forgot his aching bones and the gout that continued to gnaw at him.

Above: The *Centuries* spread Nostradamus's fame even further throughout France. This illustration from an early edition of the work shows the seer at work in his study in Salon.

THE SEER'S ROYAL PATRONS

Henri II of France was crowned in 1547, upon the death of his father, Francis I. That he came to the throne was a near-miracle in itself. At the age of seven, he and his elder brother were shut away in a dank Spanish monastery as hostages for their father. They remained in captivity for four years. When young Henri finally made it back home to France, he had to relearn his native tongue – which his Spanish jailers had forbidden him to speak – and was a shy, quiet boy who was all at sea in the loud, gaudy court. At the age of 14, he was married off to Catherine des Médicis, from the famed Florentine family. They had little in common, and Henri found solace in a much older mistress, Diane of Poitiers, who was considered virtually a second queen upon his rise to the throne. Diane was a cousin of Catherine, as was Mary Stuart, who married Catherine's eldest son, the dauphin.

Catherine was a remarkable woman, highly intelligent and considerate, but the French court never really accepted her, deriding her as 'the banker's daughter' – an allusion to her family background. She was no great beauty – which was a trait much prized by the French court – and the mean-spirited aristocrats did little to disguise their feelings about her plainness. Yet she did have one important friend at court in the years before Henri's coronation. King Francis loved her as his own child.

"Let those who read these verses consider them with mature mind,
Let not the profane and ignorant mob be drawn to study them,
Let all of the Astrologers, the Fools and the Barbarians keep aloof,
Let him who acts otherwise be cursed according to ritual."

Nostradamus pressed on with his writing despite failing health, refusing to yield to the carping of the critics, and completed work on the *Centuries*. In June 1566, knowing that his time on Earth was growing short, he dictated his will. "June 30th, in the year 1566, Maître Michel Nostradamus, doctor of medicine, astrophile, Physician-in-Ordinary and counsellor to the king, bequeaths to his daughter Magdeleine 600 ecus of gold, and to his other daughters, Anne and Diane, 500 ecus of gold. To his dear wife, Anne Ponsart, 400 ecus of gold, together with certain household furniture. I bequeath, moreover, all my books to that one of my sons who improves himself or profits most from study, together with all letters, notes and manuscripts found in the dwelling of the testator, who has not at all desired that an inventory should be taken, but that his effects should be gathered and closed up in one of the rooms of the house until the one who should have them will be of age to receive them."

In addition, he made further bequests to various religious orders and the poor. The very next day, he asked his local priest to give him the last rites as he was certain they would not meet again. He is said to have told his close friend, Chavigny, "You will not find me alive by sunrise."

Sure enough, the very next morning Chavigny found the prophet slumped over his bench in his beloved study, a victim of dropsy. In keeping with his renowned powers, Nostradamus had even penned a quatrain for the occasion:

"On returning from an embassy, the King's gift safely stored,
No more will I labour, for I will have gone to God.
By my close relations, friends and brothers, I shall be found dead, near my bed and the bench."

He was set upon by enthusiastic crowds, who showered him with applause and salutations. The next day, he was given his audience with the King and Queen, who welcomed him with a mixture of awe and excitement.

Catherine was particularly interested in the small man who stood before them. She not only wanted explanations of some of the quatrains she found most troubling – particularly those that seemed to be about her husband – but also wanted him to cast the horoscopes of her children. Nostradamus had already foreseen grim fates for the princes and princesses, but kept his counsel and travelled the hundred miles to Blois, where the royal offspring lived in a splendid château, far removed from the clamour and filth of Paris.

Rather than tell the horrible truth about what he foresaw for the children, he diplomatically concentrated on the positive aspects of their future lives. But the visions he had seen – which will be looked at in more detail in the next chapter – proved to be too much for Nostradamus to ignore. As he sat watching the children play, he began to see the castle awash in a bloody mist. The next day, he made a hasty departure back to Paris, where he stayed another month before his return to Salon.

In 1558, Nostradamus published another edition of his startling prophecies, which contained some 400 additional quatrains. Not only did it showcase his amazing talents even more, but also showed the old man was sick of the barbs his detractors had constantly aimed his way. The edition contained a bitter verse in which he cursed them:

Below: This illustration from the 15th-century Beauvais tapestry shows Paris much as it was when Nostradamus visited it for his audience with Henri and Catherine in 1555.

Nostradamus, the greatest of all seers, was dead at the age of 62. After his will was read, it was learned that he had two last requests; to be buried upright because he could not bear the thought of people walking over him 'during my final sleep' and to rest forever in peace. In keeping with his wishes, he was immured in the wall of the Church of the Cordeliers in Salon – but it was not to be his final resting place.

Final Prediction

In Century IX, Quatrain 7, he had written that death would come to any man who violated his grave.

"The man who opens the tomb when it is found,
And who does not close it immediately,
Evil will come to him that no-one will
Be able to prove."

It so happened that in May, 1791, during the height of the French Revolution, three drunken soldiers decided to expose Nostradamus's remains and test the truth of a legend that had grown up about him, that whoever drank from his skull would inherit his powers. After opening the coffin, the three soldiers froze – not out of fear of the skeleton, but at the plaque dangling around its neck. It is said to have given the exact date his remains would be desecrated!

Despite the bizarre and terrifying scene, one soldier decided to press his luck, and took the skull out from the casket. Into it he poured some wine from a bottle, then looked at his comrades before taking a long swig. No sooner had he swallowed than a shot from a nearby street riot pierced the darkness – and the foolish soldier's head. He was dead before he hit the ground!

In 1813, Nostradamus was re-interred in the church of St Laurent, where he has rested in peace ever since. Nearby is a tablet, reading "Here lie the bones of the illustrious Michel Nostradamus, whose almost divine pen alone, in the judgment of all mortals, was worthy to record, under the influx of the stars, the future events of the whole world. He died at Salon in the year 1566. Posterity, disturb not this sweet rest! Anne Ponce Gemelle hopes for her husband true felicity."

Nostradamus's legacy is an enigmatic body of work that continues to challenge us more than four centuries later. Charles Ward, author of *Oracles of Nostradamus*, summed up its appeal. "It has been well said that the man and his works are an enigma. Everything in our

author is ambiguous; the man, the thought, the style. We stumble at every step in the rough paths of his labyrinth. We try to interrogate, but grow silent before a man of emotionless nerve and of impenetrable mask. What are these *Centuries*? What is Nostradamus? In them and him all may find something; but no man born of woman can find all. The Sphinx of France is here before us; a riddler, riddling of the fate of men; a man at once bold and timid; simple, yet who can plumb his depth?"

Come now, as we try to probe the layers of his amazing visions – glimpses of the future as recorded by the great prophet of Salon.

WRITTEN ON THE SKIN

During the days he spent in Paris, Nostradamus met a 10-year-old prince, whose moles intrigued the great seer. The boy was undressed, and Nostradamus went to work. Placing a hand on the lad's head, he turned the young prince completely around so he could better study the moles. After a few minutes of intense observation, Nostradamus turned to the boy's guardian and told him that not only would the prince become King of Navarre, but that he would later be King of all France.

The prediction was met with a chorus of disbelief throughout the royal court, for it meant that a Protestant Huguenot would ascend to the throne. This was, at the time, about as likely as a Frenchman becoming Prime Minister of Great Britain today. True to the remarkable vision, though, the young prince did become King of Navarre in 1572, and 25 years later was crowned King Henri IV, one of the most beloved rulers in French history.

CHAPTER TWO

Predictions for his own lifetime

His reputation grows as his prophecies come true

During the time in which he lived, Nostradamus was celebrated - or reviled, depending on the individual's view of his writings - for his predictions concerning the French royal family and the battles and intrigues of his day.

But now, even some of those quatrains are open to new interpretations which would appear to be just as valid as those we have long held to be the definitive asessments.

Either way, there is no doubting the fact that Nostradamus was considered a marvel by those enlightened enough to understand him even during those superstitious times.

HENRICVS II FRAC... REX XRIANISSIMV
NNO ÆTATIS SVÆ XXXVII · 1555

"In the year when a single eye reigns in France
The court will be in grievous trouble.
His friend will kill the Great One Blois
The Kingdom will be thrown into evil
condition and double uncertainty."

Though these quatrains were widely believed at the time to refer to the King, Henri was not too worried about the dire predictions of death on the battlefield, but his wife, Catherine, was. During her meeting with Nostradamus in Paris, she at first hedged around asking him to explain the quatrains that seemed to predict that her husband would die a slow and horrible death, but her curiosity eventually got the better of her. After giving his terrifying interpretation, Nostradamus diplomatically added the rider that he had no power over his own visions, but that if steps were taken, the prophecy could be avoided. Nostradamus had two reasons for saying this. As a good Catholic, he fervently believed in free will, and that the future could be changed; and he was also aware that a previous astrologer to the royal court, Lucas Gaurico, had endured unspeakable tortures for having once predicted the King's death.

Left: Henri II (1519-89) succeeded to the throne of France in 1547. A man of action, he had little time for soothsayers.

Below: Queen Catherine was, however, intrigued by the prophecies of Nostradamus, and instrumental in inviting him to the court.

Nostradamus not only made predictions that revealed events far into his future and ours, but also saw wonderfully accurate visions of things that would occur before his own death in 1566. As each one came to pass, his reputation grew among the aristocrats and peasants of his own time.

His record provides us with a sombre warning. For if he was right about our past, is it not conceivable that he will be just as accurate about our future? If so, mankind has a terrifying tomorrow in store for it. Yet the great prophet always insisted that his visions of things to come were not set in stone. People could indeed change their future, but only if they heeded the warning signs that Nostradamus had left for them.

Unfortunately, Henri II, King of France, was a man who paid no mind to soothsayers. Quatrain 35 of Century I remains one of the most dazzling of all the seer's visions.

"The young Lion will overcome the old in
single combat on a martial field.
His eyes, encased in gold, will be put out.
When two are in the lists, fighting as one
He will receive a mortal blow and die a cruel
death."

Another quatrain, the 55th of the third Century, refers to the same event.

In 1559, Nostradamus's prediction was fulfilled. Henri II had recently signed an important peace treaty with his long-time enemies, the Spanish, and two royal marriages were planned to celebrate and seal the new agreement. The marriages took place in the month of June, and the King rejoiced with a lavish three-day celebration of jousts, tournaments and feasts in the French capital. It was one of grandest celebrations held in 16th-century France and royalty from all over the continent was invited to attend.

Fatal Joust

On 29 June, Henri, a muscular, athletic man who loved the sport of jousting, decided to join in the tournament on the final day. He challenged his young Scottish captain of the guard, the Earl of Montgomery, to single combat. Not surprisingly, the Earl wanted nothing to do with it, for, like the rest of the royal court, he had read Nostradamus' predictions and feared over his fate should the king die in the lists.

The dashing King was adamant, however, and commanded the nervous Scot to face him in the joust. Henri II wore his best armour – golden in colour with an intricate helmet made of gold. As Nostradamus had noted in his quatrain, published some years earlier, both men were indeed 'lions'; each of them wore the emblem of the beast on their chests. Twice they rode against each other without incident, but the third time they met, their lances at last crossed. Montgomery's thrust was deflected upwards to hit the King's neck. The lance splintered and a jagged sliver shot upwards, forcing up

Above: Lucas Guarico (1476-1558), an Italian Bishop and astrologer was put to the torture for predicting Henri II's death.
Left: In the court of Henri II and his successors good looks counted for more than ability and rank was marked by finery of costume.

Henri's protective visor, and entering his eye, causing the 'two wounds in one' of which Nostradamus had written.

Henri, mortally wounded, was carried from the battlefield as the horrified Montgomery looked on in dread over his own fate. Henri lingered in horrible agony for eleven days before he succumbed, fulfilling the prophecy of 'a single eye' reigning in France. Astonishingly, Nostradamus also predicted the dire problems that lay ahead for the young Earl of Montgomery, who was given no choice by the late King other than to face him.

"He who in a struggle with a weapon in a warlike deed,
Will carry off the prize from one greater than he.
One night, six will bring harm to his bed;
Naked, without his armour, he will suddenly be surprised."

Century III Quatrain 30

From his death bed, the forgiving Henri II issued orders that Montgomery was not to be blamed for the outcome of the joust, and should not be harmed in any way whatsoever. However, the grieving Queen Catherine gave no such assurances, and the panicked Montgomery, hearing of her threats, wisely fled to England and safety.

Perhaps he should have stayed there. Some time later, though, he returned to France to lead rebellious Protestants against the Catholics. After a disastrous campaign in Normandy, he was given the opportunity to surrender. This he did, but only after receiving a promise that his life would be spared from the avenging royal family. Catherine's desire for vengeance could not be sated, no matter what was said in her name, so she secretly dispatched six men to arrest

Below: In 1559, Henri II signed a treaty with his arch-enemy Philip II of Spain. The peace was cemented by royal marriages and celebrated by the tournament in which Henri lost his life.

Montgomery and return him to Paris. They kidnapped him from his bed and delivered him into a prison. Nostradamus does not say what happened to the Earl after this, but he disappears completely from the historical record.

Nostradamus's incredible predictions concerning the King and his family did not begin or end with Henri's death.

"Brothers and sisters captive, in varying places,
Will find themselves passing near the monarch.
His attentive offspring will look at them,
Displeased to see the signs on their chins, foreheads and noses."

Century II Quatrain 20

In September, 1557, shortly after Century II was published, Henri II took his children to see a group of Huguenots captured during one of the many raids

that occurred during these years of perpetual religious conflict. Just as the seer suggests, the sympathetic King was angered to see so many of the Huguenots wounded and battered.

Following Henri's death, a struggle broke out among factions headed by the Bourbon and Guise families, pitting Catholic against Protestant. The new boy-king, Francis II, suffered from frail health. His enemies saw him as an easy target, ripe for removal from the French throne, but did not count on the courage or guile of Catherine, now Queen Mother and effectively Regent of France.

"The Royal Lady shall dwell alone in power
After passing of her matchless husband, first on the field of honour.
For seven years she will lament her sorrow,
Then, gifted with long life, she will rule to an advanced age."

Century IV Quatrain 63

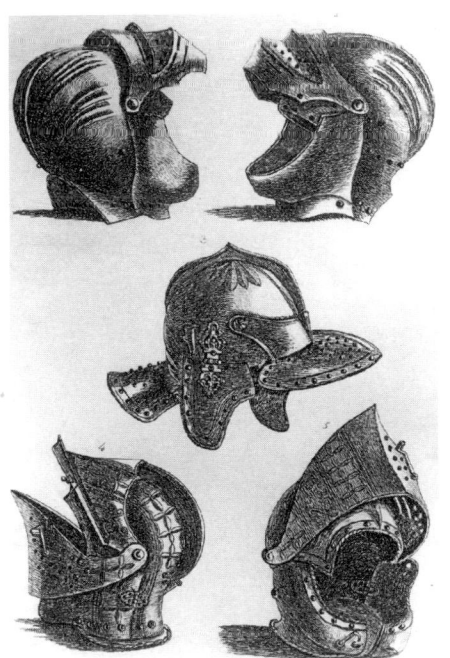

Top: A German engraving of the tournament in 1559 where, as Nostradamus had predicted, Henri II was killed in a joust with his captain of the guard, the Earl of Montgomery.

Above left: Jousting lances were blunt, and participants wore heavy metal armour, but a splinter from a shattered lance flew through the king's protective visor and into his eye.

Above right: Henri was not killed instantly, but lingered for 11 days as his anxious family watched, fulfilling the prophecy that a one-eyed man would briefly rule France.

François II.

Above: Henri's oldest son, just 15 years old, succeeded to the throne as François II, but died the following year, leaving Mary Stuart a widow.

Above: Queen Catherine was intrigued by what Nostradamus predicted for her children, but was unable to save them from their fates.

Catherine lived until she was 70, a ripe old age for the time, and especially for someone in a royal house subject to intrigue and assassination. Just as Nostradamus had revealed, she mourned for seven years then made a grand tour of France – the first time she had shown herself amid such pomp and circumstance since the joust.

Even before Henri's death, Nostradamus had demonstrated his remarkable powers to the royal court. In 1557, the King sent French troops into Italy to help the Pope in his war against Philip II of Spain. Months earlier, Nostradamus had warned Henri against such a move.

"The French army in Italy will be troubled
Throughout the conflict, and sustain
great loss.
Flee, citizens of Rome. Oh, France,
driven back
Near to the Tessin in your doubtful struggle
to reach the Rubicon!"

Century II Quatrain 72

Later that year, with Henri's forces in difficulties in Italy, Philip sent his armies against St-Quentin, one of the great fortifications of France. The Spanish, under the Duke of Savoy, laid siege to the city, under-armed because the French forces were still mired in battle in Italy.

"The great city, suddenly and to its
repentance, will be taken by assault,
Surprised in the night, its defences will be
broken down.
The guards and lines of communications at
St- Quentin
Will be destroyed, and its gates battered in."

Century IV Quatrain 8

"The fine city will be abandoned to
the soldiery,
Never was mortal tumult closer at hand.
O what hideous death is closing in,
Except one crime, nothing will be spared
the people."

Century VI Quatrain 96

The citadel of St-Quentin was, indeed, taken. It was a crushing victory for the Spanish, and France appeared humbled before the world.

Henri II, having lost one city, decided to replace it by the recapture of another,

NEW INTERPRETATION

There is another possible meaning to Quatrain 96 of Century VI. The latest thinking is that this riddle could refer to the fall of Paris to the Germans in 1940. There is much within the quatrain to suggest this new interpretation. To Nostradamus, Paris was often referred to as 'the fine city', and it – and France – were indeed abandoned by the remnants of the French army in the face of the Nazi blitzkrieg.

The reference to the 'hideous death closing in' could be considered a metaphor for the horrors of the Nazi occupation and its attendant obscenities, such as slave labour, mass executions and torture.

Calais, which had been held by the English since 1347. Calais, as St-Quentin had been, was terribly undermanned, and made for easy prey. Francis, Duke of Guise, led a French force that recaptured the port in 1558.

"The great Duke of Alva will enter the war
In a manner traitorous to his grand-sires.
The great Duke of Guise will put an end
to the war
With a captivity that shall be his enduring
monument."

Century VII Quatrain 28

Again, Quatrain 29 of Century IX:

"The country which has accomplished
nothing will give place,
It will eventually abandon what was captured
but not captured,
The Church will be on fire over the
bloodshed,
Guines, Calais and Oye will be returned."

Following the capture of Calais, there was an uneasy peace, but Nostradamus correctly saw the treaties of 1559 as a preamble to a far more devastating and bloody conflict. In Quatrain 52 of Century IX, he wrote:

"Peace approaches from one side, but war
Will be pursued on a greater scale than ever.
Men and women will weep, innocent blood
will flow throughout the land.
And it will happen throughout France."

As we have already seen, Henry II ordered massive celebrations in honour of the treaty, including royal marriages

Below: Elizabeth Tudor ruled England for 45 years. Nostradamus not only foresaw the glory of her reign, but also accurately predicted the age she would reach and the year of her death.

THE BATTLE FOR CALAIS

The importance to France of the recapture of Calais and its return to French dominion cannot be overstated. The city had been held by the English for more than 200 years, and its annexation had been a constant thorn in the side of the French aristocracy and peasants alike. The Duke of Guise became a great French hero after the successful liberation of the town. Even the Pope hailed the victory as more important than the taking of half of all England, by then a Protestant state.

Mary Tudor, Queen of England at the time, exclaimed that, "If they open my heart, they will find Calais graven on it." Indeed, the loss of Calais was a disaster for England and its queen, as vast sums of gold, munitions, cannons and merchandise were lost in its fall. The town would remain secure in French hands until 1940, when the dark hordes of the Nazi Wehrmacht invaded and captured it.

and the ill-fated jousting tournament. One of the marriages was between his sister Marguerite and the Duke of Savoy, the man responsible for routing the French at St-Quentin.

"Under the pretext of a marriage settlement, Great Henry will, comfortable to the situation, act with generosity. Quentin and Arras being recovered through a journey, The Spanish will at this time take a back seat at slaughter."

Century VI Quatrain 8

Another marriage took place between Mary and Philip, just as Nostradamus had foreseen. In Century VI, Quatrain 74, he wrote:

"The great king will acquire new relatives, Before she shall have rendered up his soul The people will see him take for kindred Eagles, Lions and Cross; in doing this he will sell out the Crown."

The 'Eagles, Lions and Cross' were respectively the emblems of Spain, Scotland and Savoy. At the time, many people believed Henry had been too generous with his wedding presents, that he had sold out French interests for the sake of peace.

"When the serpents will surround the altar, The Trojan blood is troubled by the Spanish. A great number will be decimated by them. The leader flees, hidden in the marshy swamps."

Century I Quatrain 19

Following Henri II's tragic end, Catherine decided to change her personal emblem to a star encircled by a snake biting its own tail. The 'Trojan blood' of the second line is one of Nostradamus's favourite metaphors for the French royal family, which was at odds with Spain throughout the last 40 years of the 16th century. The last line has never been adequately interpreted.

In 1559, Mary Tudor died, and the young Protestant, Elizabeth I, succeeded to the throne of England. A few years before she became Queen, Nostradamus published several predictions about her. He foresaw not only her accession but also the enormous, and politically unexpected, successes of her reign.

"The rejected one shall at last reach the throne, Her enemies found to have been traitors. More than ever shall her period be triumphant. At seventy she shall go assuredly to death, in the third year of the century."

Century VI Quatrain 74

Elizabeth I was the daughter of Henry VIII and his second wife, Anne Boleyn. For many years she was denied her royal inheritance by plotters whom she considered traitors and enemies of England. As the seer predicted, her reign was indeed one of remarkable triumph. She not only presided over the destruction of the Spanish Armada through the efforts of brilliant seamen like Sir Francis Drake, but also defied the might of the Roman Catholic Church and overran Spanish-held lands in the New World of the Americas. Astonishingly, she died at the age of 70 in 1603, the exact year Nostradamus predicted some 50 years earlier.

Because royalty enjoyed such unequalled power and importance during the 16th century, Nostradamus devoted many of his quatrains to their rules. Philip II of Spain was no exception to this.

"Within Spain there shall arise a very powerful ruler,
He will conquer the Midy by land and sea.
This vigorous man will beat back the Crescent,
And lower the wings of the people to whom Friday is a sacred day."

Century X Quatrain 95

"Sprung from Italian blood, born in the heart of Germany,
Is the leader who shall become of such high power
That he will drive the foreign Moorish people from his realm,
Returning the Church to its original prestige."

Century V Quatrain 74

As he predicted, Philip was instrumental in defeating the forces of Islam – or 'the Crescent' as he referred to them – who held Friday sacred.

A Boy King

Meanwhile, in France, Francis II came to the throne following the death of his father, Henri II. Francis had been betrothed to Mary, Queen of Scots, since infancy, and they were married in 1558, but the young king would die just two years later, at the age of 16. In Quatrain 39 of Century X, Nostradamus accurately predicted the fate of Francis.

"The widow of the unfortunate marriage will survive the death of the eldest son.
No children will be born of the marriage.
Two Isles will be put in discord.
He will die before eighteen, still of incompetent age.
The succession will be harmoniously settled upon the next of age."

Amazingly, everything the great prophet saw came to pass. Francis was indeed the oldest son of Henry II and Catherine - who survived her eldest son by some years - and he and Mary had no children. After his death, Mary left for her native Scotland and feuded with Elizabeth, which did put two 'isles' - or at least two nations that shared an island - in conflict.

"Through anger and internal hatreds,
The exiles will hatch a great conspiracy against the king.
Secretly they will place enemies to threaten him,
And his own old party against them: there will be sedition."

Century I Quatrain 13

Below: The buccaneer Francis Drake got rich harrying Spanish ships and possessions in the Americas. He was knighted by Elizabeth I in 1581 after circumnavigating the globe.

THE FALL OF GRANADA

The Islamic Moors of northern Africa have had a lasting influence on Spanish history, having occupied parts of the country for more than 700 years, beginning with an invasion in 710AD. Although Philip finally ended any pretensions they had about ruling Spain, the Moors and the Spanish had been fighting for hundreds of years before he eventually came to power. Christian victories in the 11th century ended Moorish supremacy, and Ferdinand III, who ruled until 1252, made further inroads against the Moslems' domination of his country, reducing their power to the state of Granada, where they ruled from the spectacular palace of Alhambra, one of the most beautiful royal houses in all of Europe. By 1453, Henry IV had even driven them from Gibraltar.

But it was Ferdinand II and his queen Isabella – best remembered for their patronage of the Italian adventurer Christopher Columbus's journey to the New World in 1492 – who waged the most aggressive campaign against the Moors. For ten years, they were unrelenting in their opposition to Granada, and just months before Columbus discovered America, finally conquered the powerful Moorish state. However, Ferdinand was lenient in dealing with the newly-conquered people, allowing them to remain in the country, and free to practise their own laws and religion.

The age of tolerance ended in 1502, when Francisco de Cisneros, the new archbishop of Toledo, decreed that all Moors would have to embrace the Christian faith or be expelled from Spain. Still, there was little violence directed at them, and the wealthier ones were able to buy immunity from the new edict, until the reign of Philip II. The profoundly Catholic Nostradamus praised Phillip in his quatrains for restoring the Church of Rome to its rightful glory in Spain. Ironically, during the time of the fall of Granada, it was the Jews – not the Moors – who were subjected to the ugliness of religious intolerance. With the victory of Catholicism, Judaism was outlawed throughout the entire country, and all those who followed the ancient faith of Moses and Abraham were subjected to the horrors of the Inquisition.

Left: The Moslem presence in southern Spain has left a legacy of beautiful buildings, such as the Alhambra Palace overlooking the city of Granada.

Francis was just one of the seven children of Henri and Catherine. Nostradamus had met them all at Blois during his triumphant trip to Paris. In several quatrains, he refers to the tragedy and bloodshed they will bring upon France and themselves.

In one of his Presages – the introductions to the *Centuries* – he predicted:

*"A succession of fatalities will decimate the house of seven,
Hail, tempests, pestilent misfortune and furies.
A ruler of the Orient will put all the Occident in flight
And subdue those who were once his conquerors."*

In quatrain 60 of Century IV, he wrote:

*"Seven children shall he leave behind him in his house,
The Third Estate will eventually murder one,
Two will be pierced by the sword of one of the children,
Genoa and Florence will contribute to the disorder."*

He returned to the theme in Century VI, Quatrain 14.

*"The seven branches will be reduced to three,
Death will surprise more than one of the elder born,
The two males will be corrupted to the point of fratricide,
Conspirators will die in their sleep."*

France was indeed wracked by religious wars between Catholics and Protestants, and Suleiman the Magnificent of Turkey – the 'ruler of the Orient' – had unleashed his forces throughout eastern Europe and the Mediterranean. Catherine's seven children were reduced to just three by 1575, and there was a bitter rivalry shaping between Charles IX, who succeeded on the death of his brother Francis II, and another brother, the Duke of Anjou. They became such enemies that the Duke fled France to take the crown of Poland, but he hated the country so much that he soon returned.

This quatrain refers to the abortive plot known as the Conspiracy of Amboise, which occurred in 1560. The Montmorency family and the Bourbons conspired to kill the Duke of Guise and to abduct Francis II. Fortunately for the king, word of the secret plan was leaked and the conspiracy was thwarted before it could be sprung into action. It is possible that young Francis was forewarned by his mother's knowledge of Nostradamus's quatrain.

Charles was just ten years old when he assumed power under the ever-watchful eye of Catherine. Nostradamus saw the infamy of his reign years before his ascension.

"In the year when Saturn shall be in a water sign and
Conjoined with the Sun, the strong and puissant King
Will be crowned at Rheims and received and anointed at Aix,
Thereafter he will murder the conquered innocents."

Century IV Quatrain 86

As Leo McCann notes in *Nostradamus: The Man Who Saw Through Time*, "Francis II had died in December 1560. Catherine, though de facto regent at once, did not receive parliamentary confirmation of this until sometime in the following summer, just the time when Saturn was making its ingress into Cancer, a water sign."

Religious Massacres

Nostradamus had called it perfectly. But what of this slaughter of innocents he foresaw at the hands of the young Charles IX? As we know, Nostradamus had met the young boy who would become king during his visit to Blois. Upon being introduced to him, Nostradamus turned his eyes away – for this was the lad whom he would refer to as 'the savage king' and killer of innocents. The great French historian Guizot wrote: "From 1561 to 1572 there were about twenty-five massacres, thirty or forty single murders unfortunate enough to be remembered by history. Formal civil war, religious and partisan, broke out in four campaigns marked by great battles, ending in 1572 with the greatest massacre in French history." He was referring to the massacre of Huguenots on the Feast of St Bartholomew, 24 August 1572, a week after Charles' sister was married to Henry of Navarre.

"The completion of a great disastrous action,
The name of the seventh will be that of the fifth.
Of the third a great foreign warmonger.
Paris and Aix will not remain in Aries."

Century II Quatrain 88

Of Catherine's seven children, the fifth was indeed the seventh and last king of the House of Valois, Henri III. Later, when Henry of Navarre became king of France, he laid siege to Paris in March-April 1590, the time of Aries.

Nostradamus also saw the great upheavals that would wrack Europe before his death. In Century I, Quatrain 5, he says:

"They will be driven away for a long drawn-out fight,
Those in the countryside will be the most troubled.
Town and city will have the greater struggle;
Carcassone and Narbonne will have their hearts tried out."

The Huguenot problems were well known throughout France during the time of Nostradamus, but the great struggles he foresaw took place well after he wrote the quatrain above.

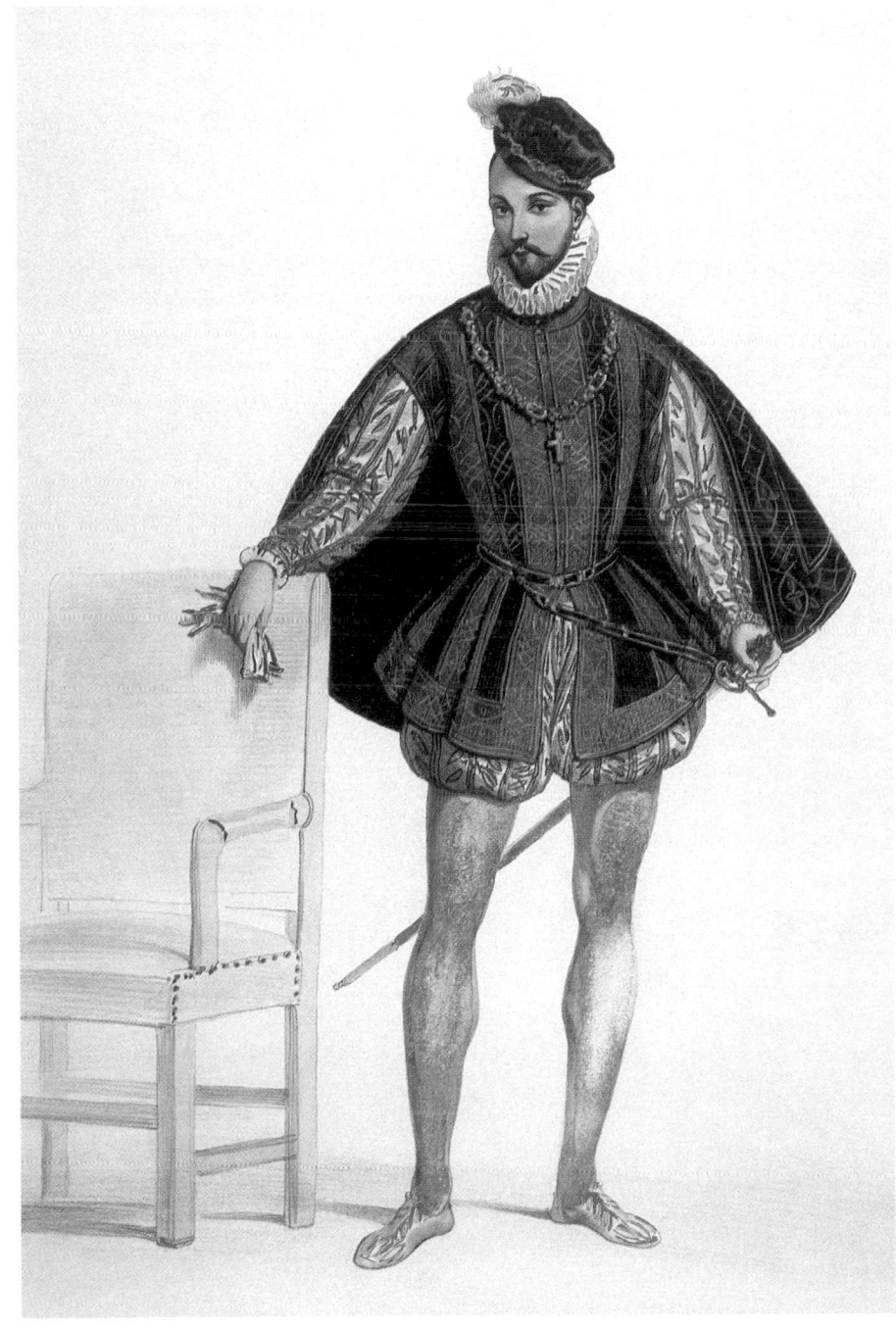

Left: Charles IX succeeded his brother in 1560 at the age of only ten. His 14-year reign was marked by massacres and barbarity.

THE ST BARTHOLOMEW'S DAY MASSACRE

The massacre of St. Bartholomew, or the aptly named Slaughter of the Innocents, was sparked by the attempted assassination of a powerful Protestant leader, Gaspard de Coligny. Catherine, who was wary of his growing power, encouraged her allies in the de Guise family to do away with him. They hired an assassin, who shot at de Coligny on 22 August as he was on his way to the Louvre, at that time the royal mansion. However, de Coligny was only wounded in the attack. Angry Protestants soon learned that his would-be killer had fled to a home belonging to the de Guise family, and a large and angry mob soon gathered outside in noisy protest.

Throughout the night and the following day, Paris was heavy with tension and awash in many rumours. On the night of the 23rd, Catherine gathered her advisers to an emergency meeting to decide what should be done to quell the simmering rage of the Protestants. During the conference, a messenger arrived with the grim news that the outraged Huguenots were planning to attack the Louvre the following day. To this day, no one is certain whether or not this was just a rumour, a fact or a plot by fanatical Catholics, but the queen was taking no chances with her life or that of her son, the king. Her key advisers told her that it would be best to strike before the Huguenots acted. Upon her agreement, she persuaded Charles to sanction it officially.

So, in the early hours of St. Bartholomew's Day, the time of the massacre was signalled by the first peal of the church bells. Leading Protestants were marked for death. They included the wounded Coligny, who was murdered as he lay in his bed, and his body hurled out of the bedroom window into the street. At the same time, barricades were erected throughout the capital, and any passer-by who could not adequately prove his Catholicism was immediately set upon and murdered. In the worsening turmoil, angry mobs sprang up to join the bloodbath, and soon there were hundreds of revenge killings that had nothing to do with religious differences. By the time the slaughter was finished, at least 2,000 people had been murdered, and their houses looted and destroyed. As news of the killings spread to other cities, similar outbreaks of violence were recorded in towns like Orléans and Lyons, where Protestantism had gained a strong foothold. Hundreds more perished at the hands of the mobs.

Word of the massacre was well received by the pope and the Spanish king, Philip II, who had long watched in dismay as the Huguenots gained increasing power in France. French Catholics were heartened by the propaganda that the killings had in fact saved the monarchy from overthrow.
However, the one ultimately responsible for the bloodshed, Charles IX, seemed haunted by it for the rest of his short life. He was plagued by nightmares of the carnage, and his screams were heard throughout the palace. His conscience did little to soften him. In fact, the two years between the massacre and his own death were marked by increasing brutality and repression.

Right: The slaughter of Protestants that began on St Bartholomew's day eventually accounted for around 25,000 lives.

"Foists and gallies around seven ships,
A mortal war will be let loose.
The leader from Madrid will receive a wound
from two arrows;
Two escaped and five brought to land."

Century VII Quatrain 26

This is an uncannily accurate account of an incident that occurred in November 1555. Seven Spanish ships were attacked by pirates, who succeeded in capturing five of the vessels, taking them to port in Dieppe.

"The sterile synagogue without any fruit
Will be received by the infidels.
The daughter of the persecuted one
of Babylon.
Miserable and sad they will clip their wings."

Century VIII Quatrain 96

During the height of the Inquisition, in the 1550s and 1560s, many people of Jewish descent, sickened by the continued harassment and atrocities visited upon them in the name of Christianity, migrated to Turkey, where

Above: Several quatrains concern piracy and buccaneering, in their heyday in the 16th century.
Left: This painting by Rubens celebrates the marriage of Charles IX's sister, Marie, to the Protestant Henri of Navarre, later Henri IV of France.

time, hundreds of miles away, Venice was being attacked by Turkish forces.

> *"Calais and Arras, help to Therouanne,*
> *The spy will simulate peace and semblance.*
> *The soldiers of Savoy will go down by Roanne.*
> *Those who would stop the rout are turned away."*
>
> Century IX Quatrain 88

the Sultan, Suleiman the Magnificent, welcomed them with open arms.

Many Jewish people settled in the great cities of Constantinople and Salonika, where they prospered and lived as honoured guests among the sultan's subjects. One such emigré, Joseph Nassi, reached a pinnacle of political power when he was appointed Duke of Naxos and subsequently became a key adviser to Suleiman's sucessor, Selim I.

> *"In the year that Saturn is freed from servitude,*
> *The Frankish territory will be inundated by water.*
> *His marriage will be of Trojan blood,*
> *And he will be closely encircled by the Spaniards."*
>
> Century V Quatrain 87

It is likely that Nostradamus is here predicting the marriage of Henri II's daughter, Elisabeth, to Philip II of Spain in 1554. It was Philip's third marriage. There was undoubtedly a huge flood in parts of France in 1554.

> *"The great pilot will be commissioned by the king*
> *To leave the fleet to attain to higher rank.*
> *Seven years later he will be in rebellion,*
> *Venice will come to fear the barbarian army."*
>
> Century VI Quatrain 75

Henri II appointed Gaspard de Coligny Admiral of the Fleet in 1552. Seven years later, as Nostradamus says, he joined the Calvinist party and became one of the prime agitators of the Huguenot Wars in France. At the same

Before 1558, Calais was still in the hands of the English, and Arras and Therouanne were Spanish possessions, so this quatrain was written sometime between the Treaty of Vaucelles between France and Spain in 1556, and the Spanish attack in 1557. As Nostradamus notes, Savoy – whose borders were less than 40 miles from the town of Roanne – was almost completely occupied by the French during this time.

Although Nostradamus saw many of the events he predicted unfold in his own time, most of the quatrains focused on dramas and people far into the future, beyond his lifetime and ours. The following chapters reveal startling prophecies about mankind's fate down through the ages – and for centuries yet to come.

CHAPTER THREE

Kings, Popes and Presidents

From Napoleon to de Gaulle – visions of power

❖

Throughout history the destiny of society has been led by those who hold positions of power. Many of Nostradamus's quatrains are devoted to the lives of political and religious leaders through the ages. New research indicates that Nostradamus saw so much intrigue and upheaval from his cramped study that he was deeply disturbed by what was unfolding before him.

Today, some believe Nostradamus even saw the mysterious death of Pope John Paul I and successfully predicted the advent of the Cold War, and its subsequent demise. Astonishingly, a new interpretation of a quatrain previously thought to refer to an influenza epidemic suggests the link between AIDS and animals. As we now know, it is widely accepted that AIDS started as a mutated virus found in African monkeys.

This, of course, is part of the inherent wonder of his many *Centuries* – their timelessness and the fact that they are constantly open to reinterpretation as events unfold.

N**ostradamus** used his astonishing powers to see far behind his own life and times. Indeed, there are few momentous events in the histories of many countries and peoples that the great seer did not conjure up in his visions. The Great Fire of London and the Dreyfuss affair, the rise of Napoleon and the Nazi-Soviet Pact, he saw them all – and more – unfold their secrets before him. This chapter reveals some of the crucial events he predicted down through the centuries, that affected not only rulers but also their peoples.

Most interpreters of Nostradamus talk of events in chronological order, but this is not the way the *Centuries* were assembled. They offer a dazzling roller-coaster ride through the pages of history, and, as we shall see in later chapters, into a future not yet made. In this chapter, though, we will follow Nostradamus's winding route through this treasure-house of adventure.

"Arrived too late, the act has been done.
The wind was against them, letters
intercepted on their way.
The conspirators were fourteen of a party.
By Rousseau shall these enterprises be
undertaken."

Century I Quatrain 7

Most analysts agree this foretells the terrible injustice that befell Alfred Dreyfus in a scandal that erupted in 1894 and soon had the whole of France in a turmoil. Dreyfus, a Jewish officer attached to the army general staff, was accused of passing top-secret military information to Germany, then France's main rival in Europe. Although Dreyfus was completely innocent of the charges – and was championed by the honourable

Alfred Dreyfus (standing) faces his accusers. It is hard to overestimate the effect of the Dreyfus affair on France, which was convulsed by a wave of anti-semitic feeling following the verdict.

writer, Emile Zola – he was nevertheless found guilty, largely as a result of anti-Semitic feeling. He was incarcerated on Devil's Island, the infamous French penal colony off the coast of South America. Life was cheap and the inmates subject to unspeakable horrors.

Secret Conspiracy

Dreyfus was the victim of an elaborate smear campaign led by his most vocal critic, Waldeck Rousseau, named by Nostradamus. Amazingly, there were, it is believed, precisely 14 men – both officers and politicians – involved in the conspiracy to frame him. The letters to which the prophet refers were the documents used to convict the hapless Dreyfus. Fortunately, those documents were proved to be forgeries. Dreyfus was pardoned and freed from his living hell on the island prison and his conviction was finally quashed in 1906.

"The lost thing is discovered, hidden for long centuries.
Pasteur will be celebrated almost as a god.
This is when the moon completes her cycle,
But he will be dishonoured by other rumours."

Century I Quatrain 25

This is one of Nostradamus' most famous quatrains, for he actually names the great French chemist who would provide the whole of mankind with a remarkable medical breakthrough with his discovery that disease-causing micro-

that his innovative methods aroused among more conservative members of the French Academy.

"The speeches of Lake Leman will become angered,
The days will drag out into weeks, then months, then years
Then all will fail.
The authorities will condemn their useless powers."

Century I Quatrain 47

After the cessation of hostilities in World War I, victors and vanquished came together to set up an organization of member nations that, it was hoped, would mediate future disputes between states so that the horrors of war, still fresh in everyone's minds, could be avoided for all time. The League of Nations – forerunner

had little power, and was only able to mediate a few minor conflicts.

"An Emperor will be born near Italy,
Who will cost the Empire very dearly.
They will say, when they see his allies,
That he is less a prince than a butcher."

Century I Quatrain 60

There is no doubt that this quatrain refers to Napoleon Bonaparte, who was born in Corsica, 'near Italy'. That Nostradamus refers to him as Emperor, rather than King, is quite astonishing. In the prophet's day, the entire continent was ruled by kings, but Napoleon did, in fact, crown himself Emperor of France! He then set about creating an Empire by conquest. In pursuit of his ambition, he devastated countries, fought battles in which tens of thousands died, and

UNCOVERING THE SECRETS OF SCIENCE

Louis Pasteur, the great chemist and microbiologist, was born in Dôle, France on 27 December 1822. Twenty-five years later he received his doctorate in sciences from the renowned Ecole Normale Supérieure. Shortly afterwards, he began to shake the world of science, producing a series of brilliant theories and experiments.

By 1857, he was directing all scientific studies at the Ecole Normale Supérieure, and began to work on his theory that fermentation was a direct by-product of the activity of yeast. Six years later, he was dean of science at the University of Lille, and had progressed to the point where he proved that airborne germs spoiled foodstuffs. In ensuing years he developed a way to destroy those germs with heat, a process to which he gave his name – pasteurization. He also developed methods of protecting beer against decomposition, and helped develop vaccines against various diseases affecting farm animals.

In 1882, when he was elected to the grand French Academy, he turned his attention to the horrors of rabies, a

loathsome disease common to rural areas of France and other countries, and became the first man in recorded history to ever save the life of a person inflicted with the dread ailment. He continued to expand the boundaries of modern scientific thinking until his death on 28 September 1895, at the age of 72.

Right: Louis Pasteur, who lived and worked nearly three centuries after Nostradamus's death, was named by him in a famously precise quatrain. As a healing scientist, Pasteur would have been of particular interest to the physician of Salon.

organisms polluted the air. This led directly to the practice of keeping medical instruments and wards sterile. Remarkably, Nostradamus also gives a specific dating. The astrological cycle of the moon ran from 1535 to 1889 – the very year Pasteur founded his famous Institute. The 'rumours' probably refer to the jealous, often extreme opposition

of today's United Nations – first met in 1920 in Geneva, Switzerland, on the shores of the placid Lake Geneva. The wonderful idea was doomed to failure, as Nostradamus clearly saw. Constant bickering between members of the 'family' of nations ended the dream of peace even before World War II buried it. The prophet also correctly saw that the League

Above: At his coronation as Emperor in February 1804, Napoleon Bonaparte crowned himself and his Empress, Josephine Beauharnais, to show he needed no authority for his elevation but his own.

eventually almost destroyed his beloved France with his constant campaigns of war and conquest. We will discuss several more of Nostradamus's quatrains on Napoleon – whom he dubbed the first of the Antichrists – in ensuing chapters.

"The divine wrath will surprise the great prince
A short time before he will have married,
Both support and credit will suddenly diminish.
Counsel, he will die because of the shaven heads."

Century I Quatrain 88

This quatrain lays bare the fate of Charles I of England. On his wedding day in 1625 – the King married a Catholic princess – he ordered that the persecution of Catholics would no longer be tolerated in England. In retaliation, the Protestant Parliament cut off his requests for further monies to continue his war against the arch-enemy, Spain.

"That which neither weapon nor flame could accomplish
Will be achieved by a sweet-speaking tongue in a council.
Sleeping, the king will see the enemy
Not in war or of military blood."

Century I Quatrain 97

The death of Henri III of France, who was assassinated in 1589, is precisely prophesied by Nostradamus, who foresaw that the king would die neither in combat nor at the hands of another soldier. Instead, he was murdered by a monk who gained access to the sovereign's inner sanctum by deceit, claiming he had an important message to deliver to Henri. As the cleric bent down to whisper in the king's ear, he pulled a knife from beneath his habit and stabbed him to death. Nostradamus's reference to the king seeing his killer in his sleep was also correct. Shortly before his death, Henri confided to his homosexual lovers that he had dreamed he would soon die a most violent death!

"There will be a number of condemned people
When the monarchs are reconciled.
But one of them will be so unfortunate that
They will hardly be able to remain allied."

Century II Quatrain 38

Most modern interpreters of Nostradamus believe this quatrain presages the pact between the dictators Adolf Hitler and Josef Stalin before the outbreak of World War II. It would have devastating consequences for world peace. At the time, no-one could believe that leaders embodying such disparate creeds could ever come to an agreement, yet they stunned the world by signing a non-aggression treaty.

The seer also foretold the instability of the uneasy alliance. True to form, he was right. In 1941, Hitler attacked his 'ally' – his greatest military blunder of the war!

New Revelations

A recent reappraisal of this quatrain has provided an alternative interpretation; it is now believed by some to be about the Yalta conference of 1945, when Roosevelt, Churchill and Stalin had a summit meeting at the Crimean resort. The first line in this interpretation refers to the Nuremberg war crimes trials,

while the third line refers to the coming Cold War between the Soviet Union and the Western allies, though to describe this as 'unfortunate' may be taking understatement too far.

> *"The blood of the just shall be required of London*
> *Burnt by fireballs in thrice twenty and six;*
> *The ancient lady shall fall from its high place*
> *And many edifices of the same sort shall be destroyed."*
>
> Century II Quatrain 51

This amazingly accurate vision foretells of the Great Fire of London, which razed areas of the city over three days in 'thrice twenty and six' – 1666,

Below: The marriage of the nominally Protestant King Charles I to a French Catholic princess in 1625 sowed the seeds of the English Civil War.

Above: Henri III was assassinated by Clément, a monk who objected to the king's attempts to seek reconciliation with the Protestants .

Below: Josef Stalin, leader of the USSR from 1929 to 1953, signed a non-aggression pact with Hitler to buy time to prepare for war.

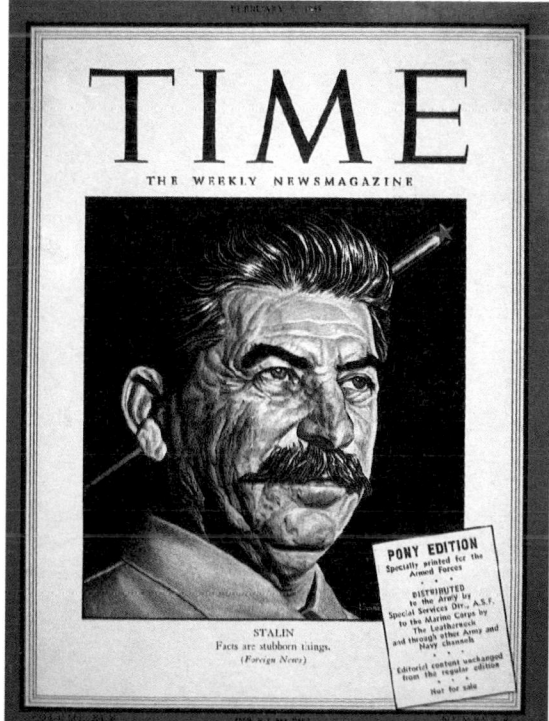

A PACT MADE IN HELL

The non-aggression pact between Germany and the USSR was the cornerstone of Hitler's plans for European domination, for it allowed his armies to lay waste to Poland and then launch attacks in western Europe without fear of Soviet interference. Stalin, for his part, needed time to prepare his country for the attack he knew would eventually come. The pact was organized amid great secrecy shortly after Stalin appointed Vyacheslav Molotov Foreign Minister in May 1939. In his first speech as minister, Molotov let it be known that, even though the Soviet Union would continue to negotiate with the western democracies, there was no reason why Moscow should not improve trade relations with Berlin.

The speech caused great excitement in the German Foreign Office. Its head, Joachim von Ribbentrop, carefully read through a transcript of Molotov's address looking for a way to improve overall relations with the Soviets. On Hitler's orders, a communiqué was eventually sent to Molotov asking him to clarify his statement. His reply was that Stalin wanted to improve political ties as well as economic ones. This was exactly what Hitler wanted to hear. If he could reach an agreement with the much-hated communists, Poland would be his for the taking.

On 23 August, Hitler sent von Ribbentrop on a top-secret mission to Moscow, where he, Stalin and Molotov worked out the details of the non-aggression pact that would stun the world. Only part of the treaty was made public. There was no mention that Hitler was now free to destroy Poland or that the Soviets could do what they pleased with Finland, Estonia, Latvia and the eastern part of Poland.

Just days after the pact was signed, on 1 September 1939, Hitler invaded Poland, signalling the beginning of the most destructive war in history. True to his diabolical form, Hitler kept his treaty with Mother Russia only until he felt he was ready to take on the awakening might of the Red Army. On 22 June 1941, with the Nazi yoke spread across Europe and the German army seemingly invincible, Hitler launched Operation Barbarossa, the largest armed assault in history, against the Soviets. He was confident of victory. One of his orders, Directive 21, declared that "The German Army must be prepared to crush Soviet Russia in a quick campaign."

German troops launched the offensive along a 1,000-mile front. Within a year, the Soviets had had six million casualties, either dead, wounded or missing, as well as 20,000 tanks and a like number of fighter planes and bombers. However, the Germans could not press home their attack against stubborn resistance. As the Third Reich devoted more and more materiel and men to the fight against the liberating allies advancing on Germany from the south and west, the eastern front finally collapsed under the Soviet onslaught. As history now knows, the bloody quagmire of the eastern front led directly to Hitler's downfall – and cost Germany the flower of its youth.

"Through many nights the earth shall tremble;
In the spring, two shocks follow each other;
Corinth and Ephesus shall swim in two seas
War arising between two combatants strong in battle."

Century II Quatrain 52

Here, Nostradamus saw the war between England and the United Provinces of the Netherlands, which ran for two years from 1665 to 1667. He drew an analogy between the English Channel and the Aegean Sea; London was Corinth, Antwerp Ephesus.

just as Nostradamus said it would more than a century earlier. The ancient lady – or 'Dame Antique' – is thought by most analysts to refer to St. Paul's cathedral, which was consumed by fire. As he also noted, many other fine buildings, including churches – 'edifices of the same sort' – were destroyed by the blaze,

which began innocently enough in a baker's shop in Pudding Lane!

The 'blood of the just' of the first line is difficult to interpret. Despite the destruction wreaked by the inferno, only a handful of people died, and some of those were thought to be the victims of opportunistic murderers.

GONE TO BLAZES

The Great Fire of London began on September 1 1666, in the King's baker's house in Pudding Lane. The great English diarist, Samuel Pepys, wrote a first-hand account of the horror. "Having seen as much as I could now, I away to White-hall by appointment, and there walked to St. James's Park, and there met my wife and Creed and Wood and his wife and walked to the boat, and there upon the water again, and to the fire up and down, it still increasing and the wind great.

"So near the fire as we could for smoke, and all over the Thames, with one's face in the wind you were almost burned with a shower of Firedrops – this is very true – so as houses were burned by these drops and flakes of fire, three or four, nay five or six houses, one from the other. When we could endure no more upon the water, we to a little alehouse on the Bankside over against the Three Cranes, and there stayed till it was dark almost and saw the fire grow; and as it grew darker, appeared more and more, and in Corners and upon steeples and between churches and houses, as far as we could see up the hill of the City, in a most horrid malicious bloody flame, not like a fine flame of an ordinary fire.

"We stayed till, it being darkish, we saw the fire as only one entire arch of fire from this to the other side of the bridge, and in a bow up the hill, for an arch of above for a mile long. It made me weep to see it. The churches, houses, and all on fire and flaming at once, and a horrid noise the flames made, and the cracking of houses in their ruine."

Left: This contemporary engraving shows the Great Fire engulfing St Paul's cathedral and other buildings on the north bank of the River Thames, whilst Londoners flee for their lives along the river.

*"The great plague of the maritime city
Shall not diminish till death is sated for the just blood,
Basely sold and condemned for no fault.
The great Cathedral outraged by feigning saints."*

Century II Quatrain 53

This is the seer's vision of the Great Plague, which ravaged London in 1665 and took the lives of more than 70,000 people. He refers to London as the 'maritime city' because it would by then be heavily reliant on trade, and be established as the home port of a fleet that ruled the seas for centuries.

Nostradamus's wrath over the 'just blood' spilled is a reference to the final eclipse of his beloved Catholicism in England in the 17th century, or, more literally, to the blood of Charles I, last English king to rule by 'divine right', who was executed in 1649. The continuing struggle between Catholicism and Protestantism was one of the great prophet's main themes.

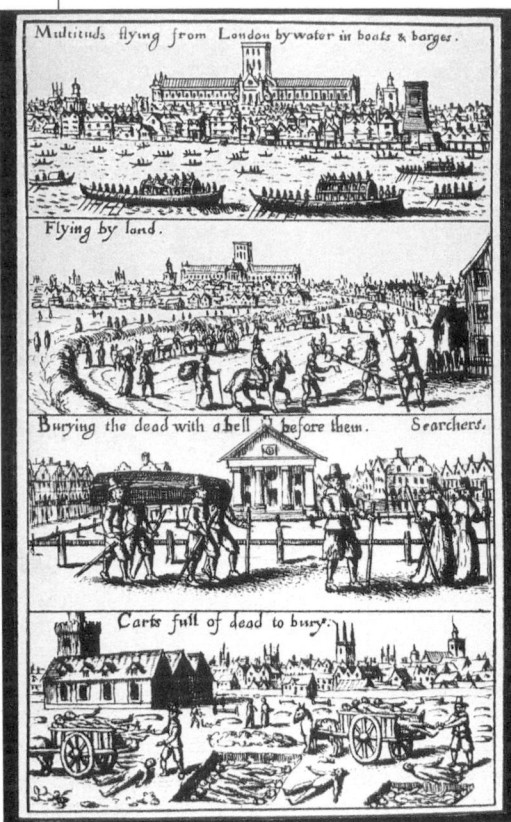

Above: The Great Plague of 1665 caused thousands to flee London. The dead were buried in great pits outside the city walls.

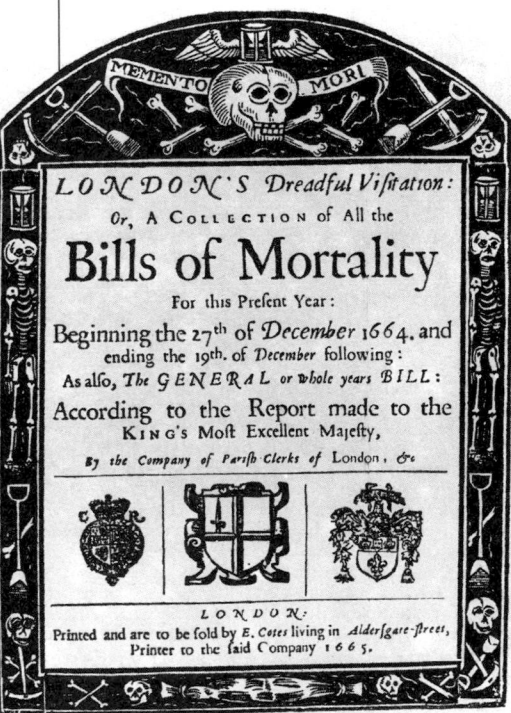

Above: A typical title page from one of the Bills of Mortality, in which the names of those who had died were recorded during the plague of 1665.

"In the Southern extremity of Western Europe.
A child shall be born of poor parents
Who by his tongue shall seduce the French army;
His reputation shall extend to the Kingdom of the East."

Century III Quatrain 35

This is another of the several quatrains in which Nostradamus reveals the rise of Napoleon, the son of impoverished Corsican parents. The Little Emperor was not only a supremely skillful tactician in battle but also a gifted orator, who easily aroused the spirit of post-Revolutionary France with his dreams of glory and power. The last line about the 'Kingdom of the East' is quite intriguing. It may refer to Egypt, where he fought a famous campaign early in his career, or to Russia, where his dreams of uniting Europe under the French banner came to a disastrous end in the bitter defeat of 1812.

Nazi Connections

A new interpretation of this quatrain identifies its subject as Hitler, rather than Napoleon. The key to this is the

Below: The body of Albino Luciani, Pope John Paul I, lies in state at the Vatican in 1978. Several quatrains suggest that his death, apparently from a heart attack, was in fact the result of foul play.

interpretation of the geographical reference. If it is read as 'the southern extremity' of Europe, then the Corsican-born Napoleon is the obvious candidate. However, new research suggests that Nostradamus actually wrote about the 'deepest part' of western Europe, a better description of Austria, Hitler's birthplace. If this is so, then line four is a direct reference to Japan, Hitler's principal ally in World War II.

"When the great Roman's tomb is found,
The day after a Pope shall be elected.
The Senate will not approve of him,
His blood is poisoned in the Sacred Chalice."

Century III Quatrain 65

"He who will have government of the great cape
Will be led to execute in certain cases.
The twelve red ones will spoil the cover.
Under murder, murder will be perpetuated."

Century IV Quatrain 11

"The one elected Pope will be mocked by his electors;
This enterprising and prudent person will suddenly be reduced to silence.
They cause him to die because of his too great goodness and mildness.
Stricken by fear, they will lead him to his death in the night."

Century X Quatrain 12

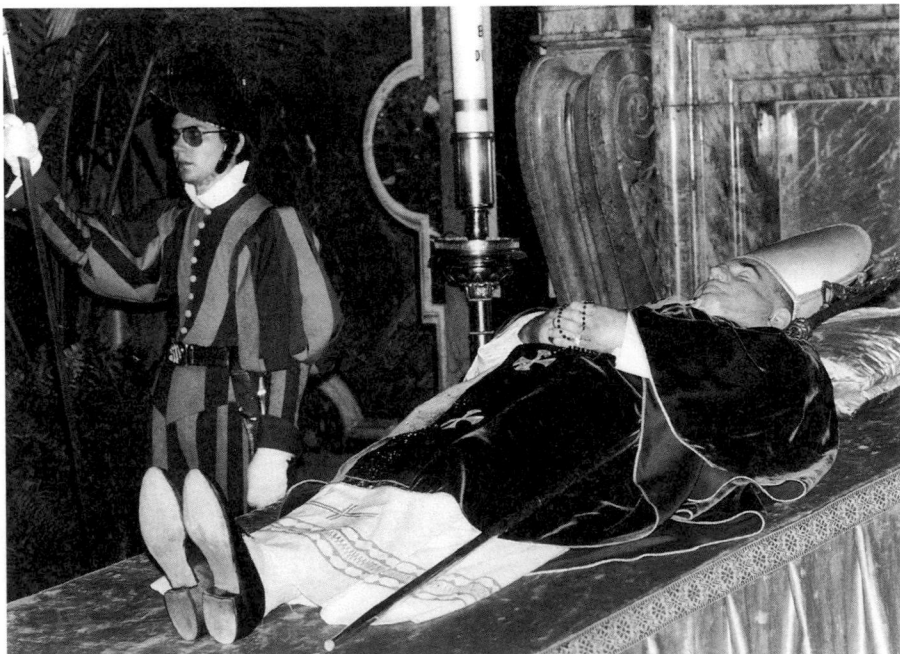

These three quatrains, it can be revealed, tell of the death of Pope John Paul I in 1978. To this day, his passing remains a mystery, and some authorities even believe he was murdered, just as Nostradamus clearly claims. Astonishingly, archaeologists found what they believe to be the tomb of St Peter, the first Pope – and hence 'great Roman' – in 1978, a short time before the death of Paul VI.

Albino Luciani, patriarch of Venice, was elected to succeed him as John Paul I. Shortly afterwards, suggest the quatrains, a number of cardinals would grow disenchanted with their choice after the new Pope begins to make widespread reforms. John Paul I was indeed a born reformer, and set about trying to change the way the Vatican did business as soon as he was enshrined as leader of the church. However, just 30 days after his election, he was dead, the apparent victim of a heart attack.

"He who had the right to reign in England shall be driven from his throne,
His counsellor abandoned to the fury of the populace.
His adherents will follow so low a track
That the usurper will come to be protector."

Century III Quatrain 80

In this astonishing quatrain, Nostradamus sees the fall of Charles I. The king was indeed driven from the throne, and his counsellor, Strafford, was executed. His 'adherents', the Scots, sold the king, who sought refuge with them, to Parliament in 1646, and he was beheaded three years later. His usurper, Oliver Cromwell, became Lord Protector of England.

OLIVER CROMWELL

Above: Oliver Cromwell, a Protestant and a despoiler of kings, filled Nostradamus with despair and loathing; he referred to him in various quatrains as a 'butcher' and 'usurper'.

Left: The execution of Charles I was a turning point in British history. This later painting is not as historically accurate as Nostradamus's written description, for the diminutive monarch died in his shirtsleeves.

SECRETS OF THE VATICAN

Albino Luciani was a true man of God, pious, humble and devoted to helping others. He wanted the vastly wealthy Roman Catholic Church to spend more time helping the sick and needy, and less on the machinations of international finance and political intrigue. Upon his election, he immediately angered the more conservative members of the church hierarchy by supporting women's rights, and his willingness to take a new look at the church's longstanding opposition to any artificial means of birth control caused an uproar. He also decided to examine the church's financial affairs – in particular the widespread whispers that connected the Vatican Bank with the Mafia and P2, a shadowy group of right-wing freemasons that numbered among its members some of the most important and powerful figures in Italy. Alarmingly, Luciani died the very day he was to reorganize the Vatican bank and dismiss some of its shadier members, including the American, Bishop Paul Marcinkus, who was its chief financial officer.

According to what we now know of the last hours of his life, John Paul retired to his private quarters inside the Vatican at 9.30pm. A little over seven hours later, his servants found him dead in his bed. On the floor were several papers and documents naming those who were to be fired from the bank. The list, which has never been published, was said to have been taken by Cardinal Villot, who headed the 12-strong Papal Curia, or Vatican cabinet. Eyewitnesses claimed that Villot also removed a bottle of medicine that John Paul used to control his blood pressure. The cardinal undoubtedly issued false statements to the media concerning the Pope's death, and ordered the body to be cremated immediately, against Catholic tradition. There could be no autopsy.

In the wake of John Paul's death, there was an enormous cover-up of the Vatican's widespread and murky financial entanglements. Several people were murdered during the investigation, including two law enforcement officers – Lt. Col. Antonio Varisco, head of the Rome security department that was investigating P2, and Boris Guiliano, the Palermo police superintendent who was hot on the trail of Michele Sindona, who ran a money-laundering operation. In the following years, Roberto Calvi, head of the Banco Ambrosiano – which had close ties to the Vatican – and Michele Sindona both died. Calvi was found hanged from a rope off a London bridge in circumstances that suggested ritual murder, while Sindona was poisoned in jail. An executive at the bank, Guiseppe Dellacha, died when he 'fell' out of a window in October 1982.

Bishop Marcinkus prospered after the death of John Paul. Although the pontiff's successor, John Paul II, was briefed on the scandalous conduct of the Vatican bank and its ties to organized crime and P2, he took no action against the perpetrators. Remarkably, he even made Marcinkus an archbishop and allowed him to remain in control of the Vatican's finances until his retirement!

Left: Charles de Gaulle, leader of the Free French Forces in World War II and several times President of France, is seen here in Algeria in 1958. He is mentioned several times in the quatrains.

"The man least honoured among the French
Will be victorious over his enemy.
Strength and lands he explored in action,
When suddenly the jealous party dies
from a shot."

Century III Quatrain 100

Here, Nostradamus casts his revelatory eye once more on the 20th century, and predicts the rise of the great French hero, General Charles de Gaulle. Like so many of his fellow officers, the unknown de Gaulle had been forced to flee to England in the face of the Nazi onslaught. There, he bade his time for the eventual liberation of France,

Above: Marshal Pétain was a hero of World War I, when he defended Verdun, but his reputation was destroyed when he collaborated with the Nazis in World War II and ran the puppet Vichy government.

gathering power and political acumen for the coming return to Paris. The 'jealous party' killed by a shot is believed to be the infamous Admiral Darlan, who betrayed France by collaborating with the Germans. He was killed in December 1942.

"The old man, mocked and deprived of his position
By the foreigner who will suborn him.
The hands of his sons are devoured before his face,
He will betray his brother at Chartres, Orléans and Rouen."

Century IV Quatrain 61

With this quatrain, the prophet saw the disgrace of Vichy France, the Nazi puppet state. The 'old man' is Marshal Pétain, the former World War I hero who so dishonoured his forefathers by kowtowing to Adolf Hitler and agreeing to lead Vichy France. For much of his time as puppet head of state, he was derisively referred to as 'The Old Man.' Interestingly, the three cities cited by Nostradamus were all liberated by Allied troops on the same day. One can

envisage the contempt with which Nostradamus viewed Pétain and his fellow collaborators as they sold France out to the despised atheists of Germany.

"Near the great river, a great trench, earth excavated,
The water will be divided into fifteen parts.
The city taken, fire, blood cries and battle given,
The greater part concerned with the collision."

Century IV Quatrain 80

Uncannily, Nostradamus is here speaking of the infamous Maginot Line, into which France poured a huge chunk of her military budget prior to the outbreak of World War II. The underground defensive line – named after André Maginot, the Minister of War who developed the idea – stretched from the 'great river' Rhine across the north-east of the country and through to the dense Ardennes forest, which was considered impenetrable to enemy forces. As we now know, the Nazis' highly-mechanized units poured through the Ardennes, outflanking the Maginot Line and rendering it more or less irrelevant as they drove towards Paris.

"Thirty of London shall conspire secretly against their King;
Upon the bridge the plot shall be devised.
These satellites shall taste of death.
A fair-haired king shall be elected, a native of Friesland."

Century IV Quatrain 89

This is another startling prediction about the course of British history. In 1689, William of Orange, a fair-haired royal from Friesland ascended to the English throne as William III, replacing

Below: William of Orange, a Dutch Protestant married to a Stuart princess, was offered the British throne when his father-in-law, the Catholic James II seemed set to relax religious restrictions.

THE MAGINOT LINE

After the brutality of World War I, France decided to thwart any future German invasion by building a line of impregnable defences along its borders. Work on the massive undertaking, which came to be known as the Maginot Line, began in 1930. Tens of thousands of men laboured on it until its completion in 1937. by which time it stretched for 87 miles. The underground fortresses – some buried as much as 100 feet beneath the landscape – were located at five-mile intervals.

At the forward edge of each, there was a series of huge camouflaged holes which were tank traps. Next came long, twisting fences made of razor-sharp barbed wire and pillboxes where machine-gunners could set up a murderous crossfire. Behind the pillboxes were rows of gun emplacements, guarded by concrete walls up to 10 feet thick. There were also numerous observation posts which gave unobstructed views of the surrounding countryside.

Inside each of these massive forts, as many as 1,200 men were stationed at any given time. There was a hospital, a guard room, stores, sleeping barracks, ammunition stocks and a mess. The forts were linked by an amazing series of underground railroads, which would be used to ferry reinforcements and supplies in time of danger. However, the £150,000,000 spent on the Maginot line was wasted, as it was outflanked by the fast-moving German panzer divisions that crashed through the Forest of the Ardennes to the north.

the Catholic sympathizer James II.

The prediction is all the more remarkable given that, in the time Nostradamus lived, the chances of a foreign-born king sitting on the English throne were non-existent. Yet, 120 years later, the impossible came to pass! Historians generally agree that some 30 to 50 English Protestant noblemen organized the successful plot against James II, the second son of Charles I.

"The elder sister of the British Isles
Will be born fifteen years before her brother,
Because his promise proves to be true,
She will succeed to the kingdom of Balance."

Century IV Quatrain 96

Above Right: The extraordinary series of fortifications which made up the Maginot line proved useless in 1940, but were remanned in 1944 after the Nazis were pushed back out of France.

Right: The gun emplacements, forts and observation points along the Maginot line were all linked by tunnels. Stores and ammunition were ferried back and forth via an underground railway.

Above: Pope Paul VI, seen here on a pilgrimage to the Holy Land in 1964, kept the Catholic Church on a conservative course during the liberal and reformist decade of the 1960s.

In this quatrain, Nostradamus predicts the American Revolution of 1776. The 13 American colonies are the 'elder sister', born 15 years before 'her brother', the First French Republic. He correctly saw that the American Congressional Army under George Washington would triumph over the overstretched English and, with French help, would 'succeed to the kingdom of Balance'. These words are a reference to America's role in the world as a superpower, balancing an often volatile world with its force of will and might.

> *"After the very aged Pope's death*
> *Will be elected a Roman of good age;*
> *He will be accused of weakening the Holy See*
> *and will last a long time,*
> *Doing controversial work."*
>
> Century V Quatrain 56

This quatrain is devoted to the succession of Pope Paul VI, who remained steadfast in his conservative beliefs during the turbulent 1960s, despite calls to change the Church's positions on issues such as abortion and birth control. Paul's 'controversial work' included taking on his old friend, Michele Sindona, as financial adviser to the Vatican Bank. In 1982, Sindona,

who had long had ties to the Mafia, plunged the church into an international crisis when a bank he controlled collapsed, an event which, as we have seen, revealed a sordid underbelly of corruption, fraud and even murder

> *"It will have chosen badly in the cropped one*
> *Its strength will be sapped badly by him.*
> *So great will be the fury and violence that*
> *they will say*
> *That he is butchering his countrymen with*
> *fire and sword."*
>
> Century V Quatrain 60

There are two interpretations of this quatrain. Originally, it was seen as expressing the growing disenchantment among the French people with Napoleon, who led them to inevitable defeat at the hands of the Russians, Prussians and British. The 'cropped one' may refer to his diminutive stature or his short hair. Long before his final defeat at Waterloo, the French had grown tired of the slaughter of its finest young men on the battlefields of Europe.

More recent analysis, and a reinterpretation of Nostradamus's original lines, makes it seem that Cromwell is the subject of the quatrain. Erika Cheetham recasts the first line as

Right: Benito Mussolini, the posturing fascist who became dictator of Italy in 1922, took the title of Il Duce, the Leader, and was named as such in a famous quatrain.

"Through the shaven heads he will be seen to be wrongly elected." If this is the case, her understanding is strong. "Cromwell was elected to power," she says, "'wrongly' in that he didn't rule by divine right.' Certainly no-one can doubt that Cromwell was a major factor in causing a bloody war of great violence and butchery 'with fire and sword.'

> *"Through the Swiss and surrounding areas*
> *They will war because of the clouds.*
> *A swarm of marine locusts or gnats,*
> *The faults of Geneva laid bare."*
>
> Century V Quatrain 85

This is another reference to the League of Nations, the world body that Nostradamus knew, almost 400 years before its inception, would be doomed to failure in its peacekeeping role.

> *"The King will find that which he desires*
> *so greatly*
> *When the Prelate will be wrongfully taken.*
> *The reply to the Duce will make him angry;*
> *In Milan he will put several to death."*
>
> Century VI Quatrain 31

Nearly four hundred years before the event, Nostradamus not only predicts the coming to power of a dictator in Italy, but also names him. Benito Mussolini took the title of Duce, or Leader. Nostradamus' remarkable

A NOBLE FAILURE

The idea for a League of Nations was first proposed during World War I by several leading statesmen, including President Wilson of the USA, Britain's Lord Robert Cecil and Léon Bourgeois of France. The constitution of the League, which came into existence in 1920, called for selective security and the settlement of disputes by peaceful negotiations and arbitrations. Any member nation which resorted to warfare would be slapped with strict economic sanctions by others in the group.

There were three parts to the League; a General Assembly, a Council and the Secretariat. The Assembly, which met only once a year, was made up of representatives from all member countries and decided policy for the League as a whole. The Council met as needed in order to settle disputes and was made up of delegates from four permanent members, Britain, France, Italy and Japan – the USA, despite Woodrow Wilson's enthusiasm for the idea, never joined – plus rotating emissaries from nine other states. All decisions made by the Assembly and Council had to be unanimous – a big reason why the League was doomed to failure.

Unlike its eventual successor, the United Nations, the League had no military force of its own, but it did have some early successes in the 1920s when it ended several conflicts – including Greece's withdrawal from Bulgaria and a bitter feud between Finland and Sweden over the Aaland Islands. However, when a dispute involved one of the world's great powers, the League was unwilling to take any effective or punitive measures. For instance, when Japan invaded Manchuria in 1931, China unavailingly asked the League for help. Later, during the Ethiopian War of 1935-36, the League's reputation was left in tatters after France and Britain tried to downplay the Italian invasion – a desparate and half-cocked attempt to acquire an empire by invading one of the few uncolonized nations in Africa – and backed only half-hearted measures against the Italian dictator, Benito Mussolini. When Hitler invaded Czechoslovakia in 1938, the League again did nothing. It last met in 1939, and was formally dissolved in 1946.

Below: The League of Nations, seen here in session in Geneva in 1926, had some successes, but ultimately failed as it had no power to enforce its decisions.

prediction also encompasses the way that several of Mussolini's opponents in Milan were sent into exile, and the fact that the Prelate, or Pope, now found that Rome, the home of the Catholic Church, was surrounded by the forces of evil and darkness.

"The warlike party, by the great Pontiff,
Who will subjugate the frontiers of
the Danube.
Those of the crooked cross
Captives, gold, jewels, more than one
hundred thousand rubies."

Century VI Quatrain 49

Here, the prophet foretells of the shame of Pope Pius XII, who was sympathetic to the fascists; the 'crooked cross' is the Nazi emblem, the swastika. When asked why he had not spoken out about the German invasion of Catholic Poland, the Pontiff replied, "There are 40 million Catholics in the Reich. What would they be exposed to after such an act by the Holy See?" Earlier, he had been Secretary of State at the Vatican, playing an important role in bringing about the See's treaty with Berlin in 1933.

"Through feigned fury of a divine emotion
The wife of the great one will be badly
violated.
The judges wishing to condemn such a
doctrine,
The victim is sacrificed to ignorant people."

Century VI Quatrain 72

In this quatrain, the prophet foretells the predicament of the wife of Tsar Nicholas II of Russia, Tsarina Alexandra, who fell under the spell of the mesmeric healer and shaman, Grigori Rasputin. The so-called 'Mad Monk' wielded amazing powers over the Russian imperial court through the Tsarina, due to his having healed her son's haemophilia. She believed everything he said without question. The 'ignorant people' Nostradamus refers to are the impoverished masses of Russia, about whom the Tsar and his family knew – or apparently cared – very little. That ignorance eventually led to the Russian Revolution of 1917 – and the deaths of the Romanov family.

> *"The great one will be born of Verona and Vicenza,*
> *Who will bear a very unworthy surname.*
> *He who at Venice will desire to take vengeance,*
> *Is himself taken by a man of the watch and sign."*
>
> Century VIII Quatrain 33

Benito Mussolini was born in northern Italy. His name means 'muslin maker', a very lowly profession in the 16th century when Nostradamus made his forecasts. Il Duce first met Adolf Hitler in 1933 in Venice, when the Führer was definitely the lesser of equals. According to a diplomat at the time who saw the two men together, "I was fascinated to watch the expressions on

THE POPE AND THE NAZIS

Pope Pius XII reigned from 1939 to 1958. Born Eugenio Pacelli in 1876, he joined the Vatican as an administrator in 1901, and his brilliant linguistic skills earmarked him for increasing responsibilities within the power structure of the church. He was the Papal ambassador, or nuncio, to Germany for 12 years, before becoming the Vatican Secretary of State in 1929. In 1933, he was the chief adviser to Pius XI when the Pope negotiated the Concordat with Hitler. When he became the Holy Father, just six months before the start of World War II, he adopted a policy of appeasement towards the Nazis, who had begun to harass Catholic priests within the Reich, and wrote to Hitler telling him he wanted a better relationship between Berlin and the Vatican.

When war erupted, he offered no condemnation of the Nazi aggression, citing 'the most conscientious impartiality', though he keenly berated the Russian communists after they attacked Finland. But his greatest shame, in the eyes of many people, was his silence over the fate of European Jews, persecuted mercilessly within the Reich. Even after he learned they were being taken like cattle to the death camps, he did not speak out, and he even refused to excommunicate Catholics involved in the atrocities.

His supporters claimed he dared not speak out about the atrocities lest Hitler turn his savagery against the Catholics held under his tyranny, but even after the demise of Hitler, the Vatican of Pius XII maintained a shoddy record in dealing with the remnants of Nazism, actively helping war criminals, including SS men, to escape to safety. It's been said that he believed communism was the greater of the two evils, and so focused more on combating it. Still, in the eyes of millions of people, that hardly makes up for his mollification of Hitler and his henchmen.

Above: Pope Pius XII, photographed here in 1951 on the 12th anniversary of his accession, claimed that his dealings with Hitler were motivated by a desire to protect German Catholics.

Left: Adolf Hitler, seen here early in his rise to power, was no respecter of religions, and harassed Catholic priests within Germany both before and during World War II.

SECRETS OF THE MAD MONK

Grigori Rasputin is one of the most bizarre and enigmatic characters of 20th century history. A peasant holy man and healer born in 1871, he almost came to rule an empire after claiming to have cured the young Tsarevich, Alexis, of haemophilia and thus gaining a magnetic hold over the boy's mother. Rasputin was also famous throughout Russia for his sexual conquests. It's been said that he bedded most of the young princesses of the royal court, and there is also suggestion he made love to Alexandra herself, but these stories are almost certainly untrue.

However, as his domination of the Tsarina grew, fed-up aristocrats resolved to do away with him. Shortly before Christmas, 1916, a group of nobles lured him to a party in St. Petersburg, tempting him with tales of the debauchery they had planned. Towards the end of the sordid night, Rasputin's drink was spiked with cyanide. Yet, incredibly, several draughts of it seemed to have no effect on the strange, brooding figure, so the vengeful aristocrats, throwing caution to the winds, shot, stabbed and beat him. One can only imagine their surprise on finding he was still very much alive, if somewhat stupefied! Finally they bound him in heavy iron chains, dragged him out onto the frozen surface of the River Neva and pushed him through a hole cut out of the ice. Rasputin drowned.

Ironically Rasputin, like Nostradamus, foresaw his own death. In his last letter to the Tsarina Alexandra, he announcd that he would be murdered before New Year's Day in 1917.

Right: Rasputin's evil reputation may owe as much to his looks as his deeds. Modern research suggests stories of his villainy are probably exaggerated.

Here, Nostradamus refers to the execution of Charles I. He was taken from imprisonment in Windsor Castle to the scaffold at Westminster, outside the great rooms of state where he had once held court. There he was stripped to his shirt to be beheaded. Later, it was ordered that the blood-stained garment be hung from a pole on London Bridge.

"A butcher more than king rules England.
A man of no birth will seize the government
by violence.
Coward, without faith or law, he will bleed
the earth.
The hour approaches me so near that I
breathe with difficulty."

Century VIII Quatrain 76

their faces. Beneath the obligatory cordiality, I found I could see an expression of amusement in Mussolini's eyes and of resentment in Hitler's." But Hitler, the man of sign – the swastika – did get his revenge when Mussolini's Italy later became little more than a puppet to the whims of the Third Reich.

"The fortress near the Thames will fall
When the King is locked up inside,
He will be seen in his shirt near the bridge
One confronting death then barred in
the fort."

Century VIII Quatrain 37

There is nothing ambiguous about this prediction concerning the rise of Oliver Cromwell. The great seer rarely injected his own feelings into his quatrains, but in this one there is no doubt that he looked upon Cromwell with grave fear and revulsion.

Charles Ward vividly recreates the moment of vision in *Oracles of Nostradamus*. "There appears to have

"The blood of innocents, widow and virgin,
With many evils committed by the Great Red One,
Holy images placed over burning candles,
Terrified by fear, none will be seen to move."

Century VIII Quatrain 80

This quatrain predicts events soon after those foretold in Century VI, Quatrain 72. It forecasts the murders of

Tsar Nicholas and his family after the 'Great Red One' – which may refer to Lenin or to Bolshevism in general – came to power in the October Revolution in 1917. The 'blood of innocents' refers either to the slaughter of the Tsar's children, or to the millions who died under the oppressive communist regime. Among the many radical policies introduced by Lenin and the Bolsheviks was the systematic destruction of religious freedom and persecution of the faithful; this would account for the seer's reference to the burning of holy images.

The last line suggests that all the Romanov family were murdered, which means that Anna Anderson, the woman who long claimed to be the Princess Anastasia – and incidentally the heir to the dynasty's supposed great wealth – was a fake. Interestingly, DNA analyses carried out more than 400 years after Nostradamus's death provided compelling evidence that Anna Anderson was not, after all, Anastasia, but an impostor.

"Far distant from his realm, sent out on a
dangerous journey
He will lead a great army and keep it
for himself,
The king will hold his nation hostage
He will plunder the whole country on
his return."

Century VIII Quatrain 92

Left: V I Lenin was founder of the Russian Communist Party and leader of the Bolshevik faction that took power after the October Revolution in 1917.

Below: Tsar Nicholas II (left) abdicated in February 1917. After the October Revolution, he and his family, including his heir, the Tsarevich (centre), were taken to a house in Ekaterinburg, where they were all murdered the following year.

been visually present to him the butcher-like face of Cromwell, with its fleshy conch and hideous warts. This seems to have struck him with such a sense of vividness and horror that he is willing to imagine that the time is very near at hand. A full century had, however, to elapse, but he sighs with a present shudder, and the blood creeps."

It's interesting to note that Nostradamus refers to Cromwell as a coward, though he was said to be quite fearless in battle. However, the prophet may have been alluding to the fact that Cromwell was so terrified of being assassinated by one of his many enemies that he habitually wore an undervest that was made of chain mail.

Here is the foretelling of the coming of Mao Tse Tung, the man who became a demi-god in Communist China. The 'dangerous journey' is Mao's Long March, in which he led his rebel armies on a 6,000-mile trek through mainland China to escape the nationalist forces of Chiang Kai-Shek, who tried to encircle them. As Nostradamus predicted, Mao kept the great army for himself once he finally defeated Kai-Shek in 1949, driving him to exile in Taiwan. Neither can there be any room for doubt in the prophet's vision of a China corrupted by Mao and his followers, from the bloody Cultural Revolution to the massacre of student protesters at Tiananmen Square.

"They will come to put the just man wrongfully to death,
Publicly in the midst he is extinguished.
So great a plague will be born in this place,
That the judges will be forced to flee."

Century IX Quatrain 11

This is another reference to the execution of Charles I, who was beheaded in 1649. What is particularly interesting about this quatrain is that the second half mentions the Great Plague of London, which occurred 16 years later. That Nostradamus should link the two comes as no great surprise. He was a true believer in the divine right of kings, and believed the pestilence to be the vengeful wrath of God striking down those who had struck down the king.

"From Castel Franco will bring out the assembly,
The ambassadors will not agree and cause a schism.
The people of Riviera will be in the crowd,
And the great man will be denied entry into the great Gulf."

Century IX Quatrain 16

In this quatrain, Nostradamus names General Franco, the long-time dictator of Spain, as well as Primo de Rivera, who led a successful military revolt in 1923. The 'schism' is probably a reference to the long, bloody Civil War that brought Franco, aided by the dictators of Germany and Italy, to power. It is estimated that nearly 600,000 Spaniards died in the fighting between 1936 and 1939.

"Ghent and Brussels will march past Antwerp,
The Senate at London will put their King to death;
Salt and wine will be applied contrawise,
So that they will set the whole kingdom in disarray."

Century IX Quatrain 49

This foretells the execution of Charles I in 1649, a year when, as predicted, war raged in the Low Countries. Parliament ordered the execution of the king. Salt and wine are metaphors commonly used by Nostradamus for force and wisdom.

"The dreadful war which is prepared in the west,
The following year pestilence will come
So horrible that neither young, nor old, nor animal will survive.
Blood, fire, Mercury, Mars, Jupiter in France."

Century IX Quatrain 55

We shall discuss World War I and other great conflicts in much greater detail in ensuing chapters, but this quatrain is highlighted by its similarity to Quatrain 11 of the same Century in that it has two predictions. The first line speaks of the great conflagration in the west, or Western Front. The remainder refers to the great influenza outbreak which devastated much of Europe as the war came to an end. In fact, more than 18 million people died as a result of the contagion, more than perished in the war itself. The last line is a reference to an astrological event, revealing when the prediction will be fulfilled.

Recently, some authorities have suggested that the 'pestilence' is AIDS rather than influenza, pointing for evidence to the reference to 'animals' in the third line. AIDS is believed to have originated in the mutation of a virus that affects African monkeys, while influenza does not affect animals. However, all the other indicators – the 'war' and the astrological data - make a nonsense of this idea.

> "The kingdom is taken, the king will plot
> While the lady is taken to death by these sworn by lot.
> They will refuse life to the queen's son
> And the mistress suffers the same fate as the wife."
>
> Century IX Quatrain 77

SLAUGHTER IN SPAIN

As the 1930s dawned in Spain, violence and cruelty were facts of political life. Faction fought faction on the streets of Madrid, Barcelona and other key cities. There was a great deal of inequality in Spanish society. In one large section of rural Spain, 7,000 landlords – who preferred life in the cities – controlled almost 60 per cent of the agricultural land. By comparison, millions of peasants bareley subsisted.

As the potential for a mass uprising grew stronger, King Alfonso XIII agreed to hold general elections in 1931. These created a Republican form of government, but failed to put an end to the bloodshed. In fact, by 1935, there was a huge schism in Spain, with leftists and trade unionists pitted against a loose coalition of army leaders, monarchists and Roman Catholic groups. In February 1936, another general election was called. The left was again returned to power, but the warring factions were not about to renounce violence. A number of political assassinations rocked the fragile democracy. The murder of Jose Calvo Sotelo, the parliamentary leader of the rightist groups, on 13 July, brought an immediate call – from some quarters – for the army to seize power. General Franco heard the call, but his initial onslaught against the government was thwarted by loyalist troops. Realising he had to act fast or become a footnote in history, he appealed to Mussolini and Hitler for help. The two fascist leaders were only too willing to give it.

Experts find this one of the most interesting of Nostradamus's visions, because it reveals telling details of the death of Louis XVI and the tyranny of the French Revolution. Erika Cheetham sums up the quatrain. "After the royal family's imprisonment, Louis XVI was executed in 1793. He was condemned by the convention who elected these powers to itself. However, the queen, who was not executed until the following October, had a newly-created Revolutionary tribunal elected to judge her, which was selected by lot. This was an institution unknown to France in Nostradamus's day. The third line tells the fate of Louis XVII. Whether he

Above: The civil war, with its savage fighting, air raids and civilian casualties, was a foretaste of World War II.
Right: A Republican propaganda poster proclaims tanks as the 'Vehicles of Victory'.

died or lived abroad is irrelevant; his kingdom was denied to him. Finally, the most interesting line of all. While the queen was imprisoned in the Concièrgérie, the old mistress of Louis XV, Madame du Barry, was taken for a while to the prison of Sainte Pelagie."

feu
tancs... tancs... tancs...
QUE SON ELS VEHICLES DE LA VICTORIA

THE REVOLUTIONARY KING

Even though he was a direct descendant of Louis XIII, Louis Philippe was a flamboyant supporter of the French Revolution. He voted in favour of Louis XVI's execution, and took the name of Louis Egalité (Equality). In 1792, his commanding officer in the army was involved in an unsuccessful plot to return the monarchy, and as a result Louis spent more than 20 years in exile. When he returned, Charles X gave him huge compensation for the lands he had lost during the revolution, and he became one of the wealthiest and most powerful men in France.

After the July Revolution of 1830, he was proclaimed King by the parliament. The early years of his reign were marked by cautious social policies, including great advances in education and labour laws, but when street riots erupted, his popularity nose-dived. For the next several years, he was largely a distant figure-head, wilfully ignorant of the economic plight of his people and seemingly unwilling to listen to the constant cries for change. The lessons of the Revolution of 1789 appeared to have been lost on him.

In February 1848, a rally of students and disaffected workers – half the working class of Paris had no jobs – turned ugly when barricades were set up to contain them. Troops opened fire on the increasingly agitated mob, and killed 52 people. The news of the massacre blazed through Paris, leading to a vast popular uprising against the government, in which the police and army joined. Louis Philippe, remembering the fate of Louis XVI, fled the country for England, where he died two years later.

"Fortune will favour Philip for seven years;
He will beat down the exertions of the Arabs.
Then in the middle a perplexing and
paradoxical affair.
Young Ogmios will destroy his stronghold."

Century IX Quatrain 89

Louis Philippe, Duke of Orléans, came to the French throne in the revolution of 1830, and reigned for some 18 years. During the first seven years of his rule, France undeniably enjoyed a prosperity and peace it has rarely known. Moreover, Louis Philippe had a rousing success in Algeria, bringing him even greater glory than his domestic achievements. In 1838, however, things changed for France, and for Louis Philippe, when ugly street riots broke out in Paris, Lyon and other major centres over voting rights – which were strictly limited. Opposition to his rule rallied to the banner of Louis Napoleon Bonaparte, whose parents were the dead Emperor's brother, Louis, and stepdaughter, Hortense. Nostradamus refers to him as Ogmios, after Ogmion, the Celtic god of eloquence and poetry –

Louis was a prolific writer and talker.

Even though Louis Philippe had his rival thrown into prison, he eventually lost the nation to him. By 1848, just about everyone in France had had enough of Louis Philippe, and when the revolution broke out, he knew it was just a matter of time before he would have to give up the crown.

"Not wanting to consent to divorce,
Afterwards recognised as unworthy,
The king of the islands will be forced to flee,
And one put in his place who has no sign
of kingship."

Century X Quatrain 22

Without a doubt, this tells clearly of the crisis that hit the British monarchy in the 1930s, when Edward VIII refused to part with the love of his life, the American divorcée Wallis Simpson. As the whole world watched the intrigue between the King and the government unfold, Edward did the unthinkable; he renounced his right to the throne and abdicated on 11 December 1936, sending the Empire reeling. As a result, he was forced to leave Britain – where the establishment continued to look down upon Mrs Simpson – and went to France, where he lived out his days in exile.

His younger brother was crowned King George VI. It's clear that Nostradamus was no great fan of George VI, seeing 'no sign of kingship' in him. As John Hogue points out, "Perhaps he disliked the new king's stutter which he 'heard' in visions. But even the Queen Mother reportedly believed her husband was never quite prepared for the sudden burden of leadership, which might have caused his premature demise." Indeed, she never forgave her brother-in-law for the strife he had caused her husband. Even George himself wrote in his diary: "I broke down and sobbed like a child. I'm only a naval officer, it's the only thing I know."

"The young heir to the British realm
Which his dying father had recommended
to him,
When the latter is dead, London will dispute
with him,
And from the son, the realm is
demanded back."

Century X Quatrain 40

Below: Following his abdication, Edward VIII became Duke of Windsor. He went into exile and married Mrs Simpson in a French château on 3 June 1937. The couple never again lived in Britain.

THE ABDICATION CRISIS

Mrs Wallis Simpson was not as keen for Edward VIII to surrender his birthright as sovereign as he was. Indeed, just days before the abdication, she released a statement declaring that she had "invariably wished to avoid any action or proposal which would hurt or damage His Majesty or the Throne. Today, her attitude is unchanged and she is willing, if such action would solve the problem, to withdraw from a situation that has been rendered both unhappy and untenable."

What she spoke of publicly, she also expressed in her private letters to Edward. "Think only of your position and duties, and do not consider me." Even after Edward's death, Simpson maintained she had never wanted him to abdicate the crown, "but nobody could make David do anything he didn't want to do, or stop him from doing what he wished. I begged David not to abdicate, begged him not to do it. I would have gone back to America. But he loved me. He really loved me."

Of that there was no doubt. As the calls for his decision grew louder, the King knew he had but one choice to make – life with Simpson. "His mind was made up,' remarked Prime Minister Stanley Baldwin, "and those who know His Majesty will know what that means."

On December 7, Edward met with his younger brother, the Duke of York, to inform him of his decision. "I found him pacing up and down the room, and he told me his decision that he would go," the Duke wrote in his diary. Three days later, in the presence of his three brothers, two lawyers and some courtiers, he signed the formal Instrument of Abdication, ending his 325-day reign as sovereign. The following night, in a radio address carried throughout the Empire and beyond, the new Duke of Windsor tried to explain why he had made such a drastic decision.

"At long last," he began, "I am able to say a few words of my own. I have never wanted to withhold anything, but until now it has not been constitutionally possible for me to speak. A few hours ago, I discharged my last duty as King and Emperor, and now that I have been succeeded by my brother, the Duke of York, my first words must be to declare my allegiance to him. This I do with all my heart.

"You all know the reasons which have impelled me to renounce the throne. But I want you to understand that in making up my mind I did not forget the country or the Empire which as Prince of Wales, and lately King, I have for 25 years tried to serve. But you must believe me when I tell you that I have found it impossible to carry the heavy burden of responsibility and to discharge my duties as King as I would wish to do without the help and support of the woman I love."

Right: King Edward's abdication speech in December 1936 was perhaps the most dignified act of his short reign.

This is another clear prophecy foretelling of the death of King George V and the fleeting reign of Edward VIII. Though British politicians supposedly objected to Mrs Simpson because she was a divorcée and a foreigner, these problems might have been overcome. However, she was also a fascist, an avowed admirer of Hitler and Mussolini.

"England the Pempotam will rule the great empire
Of the waters for more than 300 years.
Great armies will pass by sea and land;
The Portuguese will not be satisfied."

Century X Quatrain 100

Researchers generally agree that this refers to the British Empire, which indeed ruled the waves for 'more than 300 years', from the reign of Elizabeth I to this century. At its height, the empire was the greatest in the history of mankind, and stretched from Europe to the Americas, Asia, Australia and Africa.

Nostradamus calls England the Pempotam, a word derived from the Greek word *pan*, which means all, and the Latin *potens*, which means powerful. Portugal was England's great rival for a while, but she never approached the might or majesty of the British Empire. Interestingly this, the hundredth quatrain of the tenth century, was the last that Nostradamus published.

CHAPTER FOUR

War and Warfare

Battles up to the millennium ... and beyond

◆

It is no surprise that Nostradamus devoted many of his quatrains to warfare. After all, the last 500 years of man's existence have been chequered with conflict and armed combat which have taken a satanic toll on the innocent. There is no doubt that he saw all of the great battles of those centuries...and even the more terrifying ones which are yet to come.

The latest research also indicates that he predicted more wars than was previously thought. The list now includes the dog fights over the battlefields of World War I France, the Battle of Britain, the fall of the Berlin Wall, and the rise of Iranian despot Saddam Hussein.

And it is certain that he witnessed the bloody conflict of the great war yet to come. Indeed, his visions of World War III have recently ben reassessed to suggest the conflict could begin in the former Yugoslavia.

But Nostradamus often offers more than one prediction within the same quatrain. For example, a quatrain that was previously thought only to refer to the Nazi invasion of Poland in 1939 has now been reassessed, and is thought to refer in its second half to the problems in the Royal House of Windsor in Great Britain.

When Nostradamus sat down to his nightly studies of the future, he saw worlds wracked by disease, famine, upheaval and catastrophe. He also saw war, that constant companion of man since the earliest days of the Egyptian empire. Many of his quatrains are devoted to the bloodshed of battle, great confrontations between men and their machines of death.

This chapter examines some of his most astonishing predictions regarding wars over the centuries, from the French Revolution to World War III. Yes, Nostradamus predicts there will be a third war involving all the nations of the Earth, one that will threaten the very existence of man. And if he was right about other wars – and as we shall see, he certainly was – may not he also be correct about the great conflagration to come? Only time can tell.

Bloody Revolution

Unlike the previous chapter, however, we will look at the wars he spoke of in chronological order, beginning with the cataclysm of the French Revolution, which erupted on 14 July 1789 when a mob stormed the Bastille Prison in Paris, a hated symbol of royal intolerance and cruelty.

*"Coins depreciated by the spirit of
the kingdom
People will be stirred up against their king.
New saints make peace, holy laws
become worse
Paris was never in such great trouble."*

Century VI Quatrain 23

Here Nostradamus refers to the philosophers of liberty such as the writers Jean-JacquesRousseau and Voltaire as 'new saints' – the leaders of a new religion dedicated to reason. As he points out, though, the Age of Reason led to the Reign of Terror, when Paris would see untold bloodshed and strife.

*"From the enslaved people, songs, chants
and demands,
The Princes and Lords are held captive
in prisons;
In the future by such headless idiots
These will be taken as divine utterances."*

Century I Quatrain 14

There is no mistaking the vision here. In revolutionary France, the aristocrats were rounded up and thrown into prisons to await their date with Madame Guillotine while the frenzied mobs crowded the streets singing their beloved anthem, the *Marseillaise*.

*"By night he will come by the forest of Reines
A married couple, devious route,
Queen white stone: a monk-king in grey
in Varennes
Elected Cap, causes tempest, fire and
bloody slicing."*

Century IX Quatrain 20

This is an unmistakable vision of the attempted flight of Louis XVI and Marie Antoinette from Paris on 20 June 1791. The King's route did indeed take him past the forest of Reines, and Louis was disguised in a monk's grey habit when he was recaptured by revolutionary forces in Varennes.

*"By great discord the whirlwind will tremble
Broken accord, lifting the head to heaven,
Bloody mouth will swim with blood;
The face once anointed with milk and honey
lays in the soil."*

Century I Quatrain 57

Nostradamus, who referred to the French Revolution as a 'whirlwind' in several other quatrains, foresees in this prophecy the death by guillotine of Louis XVI. On the morning of 21 January 1793, the deposed king was bound hand and foot and taken by cart to the scaffold, where a large jeering crowd had gathered to watch his execution. The 'broken accord' of which Nostradamus speaks was the king's attempted flight to freedom despite his pledge to remain in Paris after his downfall. Just before Louis was placed under the guillotine, he began reciting a passage from the Third Psalm: "Thou, oh Lord, are my Glory, and lifter of my head."

Left: On 14 July 1789, the storming of the Bastille, an ancient Parisian citadel used for the confinement of political prisoners, by angry mobs marked the beginning of the dramatic and bloody French Revolution.

Below: If the destruction of a symbol of tyranny marked the beginning of the Revolution, the execution of Louis XVI in La Place de la Révolution on 21 January 1794 surely marked its culmination. As Nostradamus had foreseen in his quatrains, the King's severed head was indeed lifted from the basket and held up for the huge crowd to see.

Astonishingly, Nostradamus mentions that in the second line of the quatrain. However, this could also be a reference to the fact that when the king's head was severed, his executioner lifted it out of the basket and held it up for the jeering crowd to see. In the third line, the prophet describes what the severed head looked like. Stewart Robb, writer of *Prophecies of World Events by Nostradamus*, believes the fourth line refers to both the beginning and the end of Louis' reign as king. He ascended to the throne on St Agnes' Day, when his face was anointed with milk and honey in tribute to her! Ironically, Louis was executed 19 years later to the day.

"His hand in a sling and his leg bandaged,
Young Louis will leave the palace.
At the word of the watchman his death will
be delayed.
Then he will bleed in the Temple at Easter."

Century VIII Quatrain 45

After his mother, Marie Antoinette, was taken from his presence, the Dauphin was handed over to the care of a brutal man called Simon the Cobbler, who was ordered by revolutionary leaders to humble the boy and rid him of his regal ways. They did not care whether the lad lived or died. Simon took them at their word, and repeatedly beat the youngster for the slightest infractions. Indeed, when a local doctor was summoned to the Temple Prison to examine the lad in December 1794, he found that he had horrible swellings on his knees and tumours on his arms.

Seven months after the examination, the former prince was dead. When his death was announced, the cause was given as complications due to a severe swelling of his wrist and knee – 'hand in a sling and his leg bandaged' – but when community leaders went to view the body, they recoiled in horror at the bloody, unrecognizable mass that was

said to be a prince. To this day, no one knows exactly what happened, but Nostradamus suggests unmistakably that the boy was so badly beaten around Easter time that he eventually succumbed to his injuries.

"The fox will be elected without speaking
a word
Playing the public Saint, living on
barely bread.
Afterwards he will suddenly become a tyrant
Placing his foot of the throats of
the greatest."

Century VIII Quatrain 41

Maximilien Marie Isidore Robespierre was known as 'the fox' during the height of the revolution, because of his uncanny ability to do away with anyone he considered a rival to his ever-increasing power and ego. Indeed, Robespierre was the virtual dictator of France by 1793 after exterminating almost all his opposition. He was not yet 35.

During the early days of the revolution, he was considered a humble and heroic man – 'a saint' – but his bloodlust and insatiable thirst for power turned him into a despot. "Terror," he once said, "is nothing other than justice, prompt, severe and inflexible. It is therefore an emanation of virtue." Eventually, even the hardened leaders of the people's assembly grew sick of his brutality; in a remarkable example of poetic justice, he was guillotined in 1794, thereby ending the Reign of Terror.

Erika Cheetham argues that this quatrain refers not to Robespierre but to Napoleon III, who "was certainly cunning as a fox. He fulfills line three when he executed his coup d'état in December 1851 to make way for the Second Empire."

Rise of Napoleon

Nostradamus devoted many of his quatrains to Napoleon Bonaparte, which is understandable given the vital importance of the post-revolutionary conqueror of Europe to France, and hence the prophet. In a later chapter we will examine those quatrains devoted to Napoleon's place as the first of Nostradamus's Antichrists, but for now

REIGN OF TERROR

The Reign of Terror, which ended with Robespierre's death, peaked in the months prior to his execution following a failed assassination attempt. He drafted the Law of Prairal, which was enacted by the Convention on 10 June 1794. Under its vague terms, "Enemies of the people" were defined as "those who have sought to mislead opinion ... to deprave customs and to corrupt the public conscience." It allowed for wholesale bloodshed because virtually anyone could be accused and executed. Moreover, the accused party could have no counsel nor call any witnesses to his or her defence, and the verdict was left up to a jury which decided by its 'conscience' rather than by whatever evidence might have been introduced at trial. The only verdicts allowed were acquittal or death, and most were death. In the nine weeks after the law's enactment, more people were sentenced to beheading than in the previous 14 months. Indeed, almost 40 per cent of all the nobles who died on the guillotine were killed during this period.

Above: Members of the public who were called before the Committee of Public Safety during the reign of Terror were far from safe, especially if they had any aristocratic blood; nearly all of those tried were executed.

we will content ourselves with his military victories and defeats.

"By Mars contrary to the Monarchy
Of the great fisherman will be in trouble
The young red king will take over the
government.
The traitors will act on a misty day."

Century VI Quatrain 25

As Nostradamus so eloquently puts it, Napoleon will come to power in 1799 as a result of his fame as a soldier – 'by

Mars', the Roman god of war. The 'great fisherman' mentioned in line two is generally believed to be Pope Pius VI, who will eventually be imprisoned and die. The 'young red king', is, of course, Napoleon – red being the color of war, revolution and death.

The prediction that he will 'act on a misty day' is just extraordinary. Some 250 years before it came to pass, Nostradamus knew that Napoleon would lead his fellow 'traitors' to power in November, the 'month of mists'.

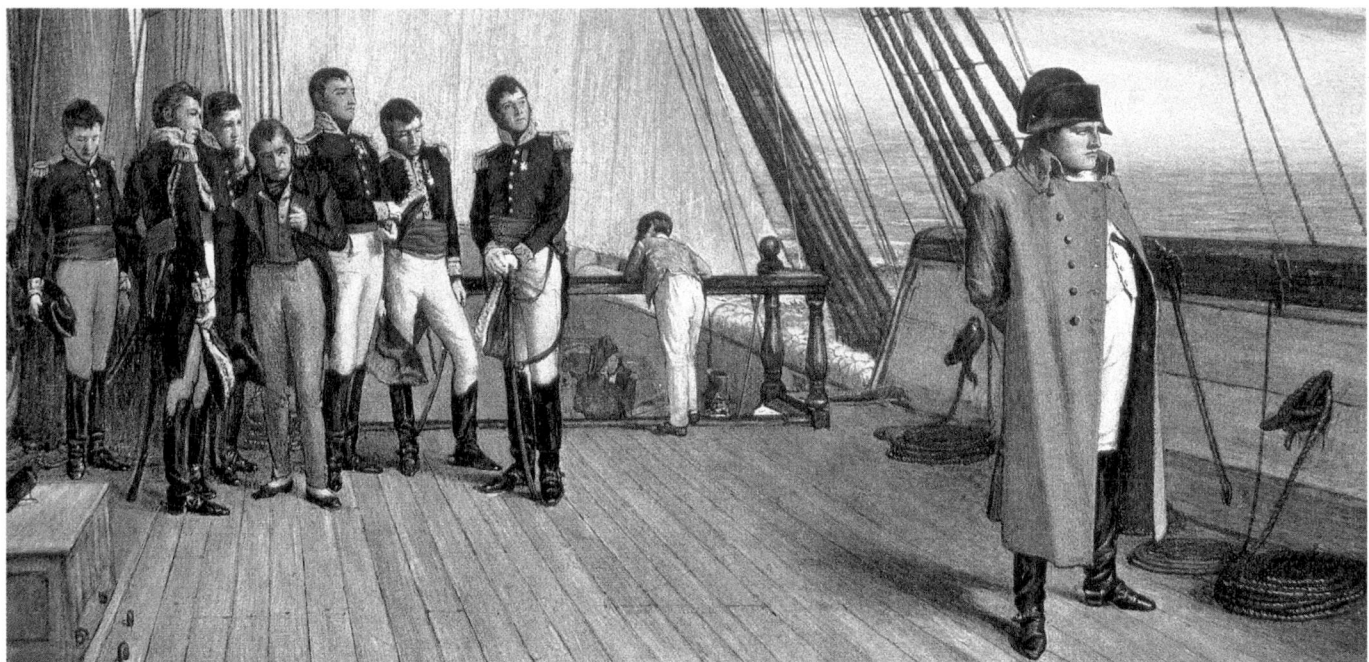

*"The short-haired man shall assume
authority,
In maritime Toulon, tributary to the enemy;
He will afterwards dismiss as sordid all who
oppose him;
And for fourteen years will direct a tyrant.*

Century VII Quatrain 13

Napoleon had his hair cut short after becoming the First Consul of France. He did this in tribute to his greatest hero, Julius Caesar. Toulon had been seized by the British and held by them for some months, until he retook the city. He did away with its government, and suppressed basic freedoms like the right to free speech. Astonishingly, Napoleon's reign lasted 14 years from his installation as First Consul in November 1799 to his demise as Emperor in April, 1814.

*"The promontory stands between two seas
A man will later die by the bit of a horse
Proud Neptune unfurls a black sail for his
own man
Through Gibraltar the fleet near Rocheval."*

Century I Quatrain 77

In 1805, the great British admiral, Lord Nelson, led his fleet against a combined armada of French and Spanish naval forces. They engaged off the Spanish coast near the Cape of Trafalgar – which stands between two seas, the Atlantic and Mediterranean. Thanks to his great tactical skills and the bravery of all who served under him, Nelson handed the enemy commander Admiral Villeneuve a shocking defeat. During the battle, Nelson was mortally wounded and died on the deck of HMS Victory, which sailed back to 'Proud Neptune' – England – under a black sail in memory of its fallen hero.

Waterloo

But what of the man who would 'later die by the bit of a horse'? Napoleon was furious with the stinging setback to his grand plan of dominating all England, and when Villeneuve was freed by the English, the emperor had him strangled to death by a bodyguard, who used a horse's bridle to do the deed.

*"The eagle, drifting in her cloud of flags,
By other circling birds is beaten home.
Till war's hoarse trumpet and the clarion
shrill
Recall her sense to the insensate dame."*

Century II Quatrain 44

Napoleon, whose legions carried the banner of an eagle into battle, was in full retreat from Moscow following the disastrous winter campaign of 1812. The 'other circling birds' are a reference to the imperial eagles of Prussia, Russia and Austria, whose armies pursued the retreating French forces back to their border. The martial music and the bitter loss of life would force France – the insensate dame – to re-evaluate the power-crazed Napoleon.

*"In the third month, the sun rising,
The Boar and the Leopard meet on the
battlefield;
The fatigued Leopard looks up to heaven,
And sees an Eagle playing with the sun."*

Century I Quatrain 23

On first inspection, this prophecy would seem to speak too generally to apply to any particular historical event. On the contrary, it does – and with the prophet's usual aplomb. It is a reference to the battle of Waterloo, fought on the soggy fields of Belgium, between the Boar – Napoleon – and the Leopard – Napoleon's name for the symbolic lion of England.

The exhausted Duke of Wellington, who had just a few days earlier fought a battle against Marshal Ney at Quatre Bras, looks towards the rising sun and sees an 'eagle' – Napoleon's banner – dancing in the breeze. Another quatrain tells what happens next.

Above: Following his escape from Elba and final defeat at Waterloo, it was decided to exile Napoleon far away. He was taken aboard *HMS Bellerophon* to St Helena in the South Atlantic where he spent the last years of his life.

"The Sun and the Eagle will appear to the victor,
The vanquished is reassured with an empty message:
Neither bugle nor cries will stop the soldiers,
In time, liberty and peace is achieved through death."

Century I Quatrain 38

During the chaos and carnage of Waterloo, Napoleon passed on a message to his commanders that the men they could see forming ranks on their left flank through the thick smoke of British volley fire were Marshal Grouchy's army come to reinforce their lines.

However, the commanders gradually realized, to their horror, that the uniforms on the left flank were Prussian blue, not red. The 'empty message' caused a great panic in the French lines, as thousands broke ranks and fled. No commander's orders or the blare of a bugle could stop the mass desertion.

As Wellington later remarked, the battle was "the nearest-run thing you ever saw in your life." After the defeat at Waterloo, Napoleon's dreams of a French-dominated Europe perished.

"From Bourg la Reine they shall come not straight to Chatres
They shall camp close to Port Anthony:
Seven chiefs for peace, wary as martens,
Shall enter Paris cut off from its army."

Century IX Quatrain 86

After Napoleon's defeat at Waterloo, seven nations drew up peace treaties through which they hoped war would be forever banished from the soil of Europe. Austria, England, Prussia, Portugal, Russia, Spain and Sweden – all allied against Napoleon – entered the French capital on 3 July 1815, and sent the Parisian garrison to Chatres.

War with Prussia

Although Napoleon's defeat signalled the end of the last great struggle in Europe for almost 100 years, there were of course great internal upheavals in many countries, as we have seen in Chapter 3, and wars between individual nations such as the Franco-Prussian War of 1870-71, which Nostradamus foretold some 300 years beforehand.

"Under one man peace will be proclaimed everywhere,
But not long after there will be looting and rebellion.
Because of a refusal, town, land and sea will be invaded.
A third of a million dead or captured."

Century I Quatrain 92

Napoleon's nephew, Louis, who would later become Napoleon III, brought peace to France following the revolution of 1848. However, in 1870, he promoted a Hohenzollern, a member of the Prussian royal house, as the rightful heir to the throne of Spain. The Prussians turned this down flat and used their embarassment as a pretext to provoke a showdown with France, their main rival on mainland Europe.

As a result, France found herself in a war she both did not want and could not win, although Napoleon was totally ignorant of the weakness of his army and the strength of the Prussians. Under Otto Von Bismarck, the Prussians and their German allies swiftly invaded France, capturing 'town, land and sea', and killed or imprisoned some 300,000 French people.

"Fire will fall from the sky on to the royal building
When the light of war is weakened.
For seven months, a great war, people dead through evil,
Rouen and Evreux will not fail the king."

Century IV Quatrain 100

THE END OF THE EMPIRE

The Battle of Waterloo was a turning point for European history. It began on 18 June 1815. Napoleon's strategy was to keep apart the British forces under Wellington and Blücher's Prussian army, allowing him to take them on separately. Wellington retreated to Waterloo to make a stand against the French after a battle with Marshal Ney. Field Marshall Blücher and the remnants of his Prussian army, which had been soundly routed by Napoleon just two days earlier, returned to Wellington's side, and together they repulsed wave after wave of French attacks until the mass desertion occurred. Napoleon abdicated for the second time, allowing for the return of Louis XVIII.

Left: While living out the last six years of his life on the island of St Helena, Napoleon dictated his life story, laying down the foundations of the great Napoleonic legend.

THE IRON CHANCELLOR

Otto von Bismarck was born in 1815, and rose to become Prussian president and German Chancellor. He was a malicious, ruthless leader who craved power and had no time for opposing views; his great dream was to unify German kingdoms and principalities under Prussian leadership. To this end, he first fought and defeated Austria in the Austro-Prussian War of 1866, then founded the North German Confederation. Now, Bismarck knew only France stood in the way of accomplishing his dream. He persuaded the various states of southern Germany that France was the real enemy, yet had to bide his time so that he would not look like the aggressor.

However, when Louis Napoleon backed the Hohenzollern candidate for the Spanish throne, Bismarck saw his opening and struck. After France was roundly defeated, the German Empire was declared and Bismarck was elevated to German Chancellor. However, he was shrewd enough to realize that even though Germany was now the most powerful nation on the continent, any aggressive moves on his part would surely lead to an alliance of other nations against him. For the next 19 years, he conducted German foreign policy with some skill, though he never gained the affection of his people because of the harshness of his government. As Hitler would do decades later, he labelled any groups who opposed him 'enemies of the Reich', and carried out severe persecutions against them. Finally, in 1890, he fell from office when he openly opposed the young Kaiser, Wilhelm II, who supported legislation favourable to workers. Bismarck railed against this as an example of the growth of Socialism within Germany.

Nostradamus as by present-day historians. In the first three lines of the quatrain, he conjures up images of massive battlefields as British troops assist France (Aquitaine) along the western front. Rain and snow turned whole regions into quagmires of horror and death, as great armies flailed about in flooded, muddy trenches.

The last line, new research has revealed, refers to Winston Churchill's risky plan to launch an all-out assault on Turkey in 1915. The allies attacked Constantinople – known as Selin in the day of the great seer – which they hoped would allow them to completely bypass the western front and attack Germany from the south. Had it been successful, the strategy could have shortened the war and thereby saved millions of lives. Tragically for the largely British and Australian forces, however, the plan backfired, and the Turks held them at bay at the Dardanelles straits.

Below: The Franco Prussian War of 1870 was one of the most one-sided in European history. A total rout and undignified stampede at the Battle of Sedan made Napoleon III's surrender inevitable.

The Franco-Prussian war lasted exactly seven months, from July 1870 to February 1871, just as Nostradamus revealed. The reference to the Norman towns of Rouen and Evreux is because they supported a restoration of the monarchy through the National Assembly and did not support a republic, as the rest of the nation did once the cannons were silenced.

The war also helped unite Germany, which of course would play a vital part in Nostradamus's predictions of 20th-century warfare. Indeed, he devoted several quatrains to both world wars, including the amazing advances in battlefield weapons and strategies.

"Towards Aquitaine, by British assaults,
And by them also great incursions.
Rains and frost make the terrain unsafe
Against Port Selin they will make mighty
invasions."

Century II Quatrain 1

The great conflagration we know as World War I was as clearly seen by

"A cannon shot shall enter within a close church.
The citizens shall be killed in their refuge.
Horses, cattle, and men shall suffer. The swelling wave will touch them.
Hunger and thirst will deplete them, even the weakest will be under arms."

Century III Quatrain 6

The German's supergun, known as Big Bertha, fired a shot that killed several people who were huddled together inside a Parisian church in 1917. Old weather records also show that tides in the River Seine – the 'swelling wave' – were very high that year.

"Fugitives, aerial warfare above the bayonets,
Sportive ravens neighbouring the conflict,
The cry goes up from Earth for heavenly aid and rescue
When the fighting comes close to the walls."

Century III Quatrain 7

How could a 16th-century man predict the onset of aerial warfare, as happened in World War I? In this and other quatrains, Nostradamus clearly saw the dogfights that took place over the battlefields – 'above the bayonets' – as armies on the ground cheered on their respective flying aces.

Some modern-day analysts believe that this quatrain has been been misinterpreted, arguing that it in fact

Right: World War I was the first conflict in history in which battles were fought in the skies, but Nostradamus predicted dogfights between the opposing fighter aces over 350 years before they actually took place.

refers to the fall of Paris in 1940. Erika Cheetham, for instance, believes that the 'fugitives' mentioned in the first line are the floods of refugees fleeing from north-eastern France towards Paris with the advancing Germans in hot pursuit. Luftwaffe fighters would strafe the columns of refugees on the roads with machine-gun fire.

"After a considerable period of plenty
The sky will touch the country around Rheims.
Oh, what bloody conflict raging around the people of this locality draws near.
"No fathers, nor sons, nor rulers will dare go near it."

Century III Quatrain 18

Rheims was at the centre of the two great battles of the Marne, in September 1914 and March 1918. Massive artillery barrages from both sides produced such a pall of smoke that the sky seemed to touch the ground. There were so many men killed around this place that officials, even relatives, could not bring themselves to visit where the soldiers had fallen in their thousands.

"The larger of the countries will be routed and out to flight.
It will hardly be pursued beyond the borders (of France).
The country will be reconstructed and a region regained,
Then all of the invaders will have been driven outside of France."

Century IV Quatrain 12

Germany finally surrendered to the Allied armies in November 1918, and France regained the territory of Alsace-Lorraine, lost in 1871, as a result.

"A bridge made of small boats will be quickly built
To attack the great Prince of the Belgians.
There will be fighting in trenches not far from Brussels
They will outstrip him, putting seven at a time to the sword."

Century VI Quatrain 81

Here we have some of the images Nostradamus saw from what H G Wells called 'The war to end all wars'. The first line is a reference to pontoons hastily made to ford rivers, while World War I was, of course, fought largely in great trenches near the Somme and the Marne and the Belgian border.

Left: The bloody, muddy stalemate of trench warfare was accurately foreseen by Nostradamus.

"Saturn in Cancer, Jupiter with Mars, a university professor, wise as a Chaldean seer, Under the aegis of a vigorous young nation, with the fullest round measure will save the country in February.
There will be the fall of Château-fort, and assault on three fronts.
The conflict will take place near Serbia. It is a mortal war."

Century VIII Quatrain 48

In the USA, World War I was known at first as the European War. America remained isolated from the fighting. On 3 February 1917, President Woodrow Wilson – an academic before he was a politician – was given Congressional approval to break off all relations with the Kaiser's government. In June that same year – when Mars and Jupiter came into conjunction – the first American troops left their homeland for the battlefields of Europe.

"A naval battle will be won in darkness.
The fight will be disastrous to the Occidental navies.
A new ruse will be employed, that of colouring the ships,
There will be wrath toward the vanquished, and the victory won in a drizzle of rain."

Century IX Quatrain 100

"The galleys will screen the ships of the line.
The grand fleeet will draw forth the lesser one.
The ships will manoeuvre to encircle the opponent.
The great navy, which is vanquished, will draw off and reassemble its scattered units."

Century X, Quatrain 2

HORRORS OF THE TRENCHES

The Reverend John M.S. Walker spoke of the horrors of trench warfare at the Somme in the book, *People at War: 1914-1918.* "Now I know something of the horrors of war, the staff is redoubled but what of that, imagine 1,000 badly wounded per diem. The surgeons are beginning to get sleep, because after working night and day they realise we may be at this for some months, as Verdun We hear of great success but there are of course setbacks, and one hears of ramparts of dead English and Germans. Oh, if you could see our wards, tents, huts, crammed with terrible wounds – see the rows of abdominal and lung penetrations dying – you meet a compound fracture of femur walking about – in strict confidence, please, I got hold of some morphia and I go back to that black hole of Calcutta and use it or creep into the long tents where two or three hundred Germans lie, you can imagine what attention they with our own neglected, the cries and groans are too much to withstand, and I cannot feel less pity for them than our own."

Left: Shells, sniper fire hazard and 'going over the top' were not the only hazards of trench warfare. Epidemic diseases were rife, and many men were sent home with 'trench-foot', caused by standing in mud.

JUTLAND

The Battle of Jutland began on 31 May in the North Sea between Admiral Beatty of Britain and Admiral Hipper of Germany. Hipper, who commanded five battle cruisers, had the initial success. His gunners found their range more quickly than Britain's six batttle cruisers, and destroyed two of Beatty's ships. But Beatty was not done yet by any means. He lured Hipper – and 16 other German vessels which by now had joined the fray – north towards the British Grand Fleet, which had 28 vessels under the command of Admiral Jellicoe. When the Germans realised they had been led into a trap, they retreated back to their base, but only after a savage naval engagement. The British lost three battle cruisers, three cruisers and eight destroyers; the Germans lost one battleship, one battle cruiser, four light cruisers and five destroyers

In these quatrains, Nostradamus predicts the great Battle of Jutland of 1916, which was the only major naval encounter between the British and German fleets in the war. Both sides were to claim victory in the battle. The Germans felt they had won because they had destroyed more ships and men, while the British were satisfied that, despite their losses, they had retained control of the North Sea, bottling up the German fleet.

In November 1918 the Allies celebrated the conclusion of the 'war to end all wars'. Just as the unprecedented destruction of the war had horrified Nostradamus, the people of Europe stood back in shock. Howecver, unlike Nostradamus, they had no idea that this was only the beginning of a century of worldwide conflict.

THE ULTIMATE HORROR

At precisely 8.16 on the morning of 6 August 1945, man entered the Nuclear Age when the first atomic bomb was dropped on the Japanese port of Hiroshima. The bomb, nicknamed Little Boy, was dropped from a B-29 Superfortress named Enola Gay. Forty-three seconds after its release from the bomb hold, the device detonated, releasing the powers that drive the universe in a blinding pink and purple flash. Gunner Sergeant George Cannon recorded what he saw from his position in the tail. "A column of smoke rising fast. It has a fiery red core. Here it comes, the mushroom shape that Captain Parsons spoke about. It's very black but there is a purplish tint to the cloud. The city must be below that."

What was below was the remnants of a once-thriving city. When the bomb exploded, with a blinding brilliance far greater than that of the midday sun, the fireball created measured a mind-numbing 540,000° F at the core, while the air pressure reached a staggering eight tons per square yard. The inferno was so hot that it melted granite stone buildings 1,000 yards away, while wooden furniture burst into flames more than a mile from the centre. But even worse destruction followed this initial blast. Soon after, huge drops of black rain began to fall. At the time, those terrified citizens who had survived the blast had no way of knowing they were being pelted by deadly radioactivity, which caused tens of thousands to die a slow, agonizing death over the next few decades.

As news of the terror spread, President Truman issued a warning to the Japanese warlords and their figurehead, Emperor Hirohito. "The force from which the sun draws its power has been loosed upon those who brought war to the Far East. If they do not now accept our terms they may expect a rain of ruin from the air, the like of which has never been seen on this earth."

Ironically, he chose almost exactly the same words as Nostradamus, who had written 400 years earlier 'The like of which was never before seen.' But the stubborn Japanese leaders refused to yield, so a second device, nicknamed Fatman, was dropped on Nagasaki, a key shipbuilding centre, on 9 August. The results were almost as catastrophic as those in Hiroshima, and Hirohito realized there was no choice but total surrender. "The time has come," he admitted, "when we must bear the unbearable."

America devoted some of the best scientific minds of the time into developing an atomic capability – code-named the Manhattan Project. The operation began after a letter – written by some of America's top scientists and signed by the great German physicist Albert Einstein, who had left behind his Nazi persecutors to settle in the USA – was sent to President Roosevelt in October 1939. Eventually, he approved the project which, under the leadership of Robert Oppenheimer, cost three years of effort, $2,000,000,000 and the labours of more than 600,000 people.

After weeks of nervous last-minute calculations, a test was carried out on 16 July 1945 at a desolate mountain range in New Mexico. As the firestorm swept across the desert plains, Oppenheimer remembered a line from one of the sacred Hindu texts: "I am become Death, the shatterer of worlds." Within a split second

Left: The blast and the fireball that followed totally destroyed Nagasaki, and left its citizens a legacy of deadly radiation.

of the detonation, men were blown to the ground by the force of the blast, which was followed by almost-deafening roar. Hundreds of miles away, people reported windows rattling, and there was a panic that an earthquake or meteor had rocked the area. Einstein, the man whose theories made the bomb possible, remarked years later, "I made one great mistake in my life, when I signed the letter to President Roosevelt."

Left and below: From his seat in the rear of the incongruously-named Superfortress that dropped the first atomic bomb, Gunner Cannon watched the sinister mushroom cloud rise over Hiroshima.

Just 18 years after the Armistice, the Spanish Civil War began, and both Mussolini and Hitler sent troops and weapons to support the right-wing military faction led by General Franco as he battled the left-wing loyalists. King Alfonso XIII was forced to flee the country.

*"In the southernmost part of Spain, the standard will be raised
And will go out to the end and the confines of Europe.
The revolution will touch closely the bridgehead at the Aisne.
It will be defeated by the great expedition of a coalition."*

Century X Quatrain 48

After three years of bitter fighting, the Loyalist resistance to Franco collapsed in 1939, a few months before the outbreak of World War II. Many historians believe the Spanish Civil War laid the foundation for the coming conflict, when the 'standard' of fascism flew throughout 'the confines of Europe'.

The advent of World War II was clearly seen by Nostradamus, who recoiled in horror at the new levels of savagery and destruction revealed to him. It is easy to imagine him, sitting quietly in the peace of his study in 16th-century France, watching with wonder and despair as concentration camps, the razing of entire cities and atomic war paraded before his weary eyes.

Above: Aerial warfare was an utterly alien concept in the 16th century, yet Nostradamus clearly saw the fighters and bombers struggling for supremacy of the skies in World War II.

*"They will think they have seen the sun at night
When they see the half-pig man.
Noise, chants, battles seen fought in the sky
The brute beast will be heard talking."*

Century I Quatrain 64

Most historians believe this quatrain predicts the Battle of Britain. There is no doubt that Nostradamus sees a terrifying vision of war being waged in the heavens, which is a stunning prediction given that he died in the 16th century! His reference to 'half-pig man' is also revealing. Look closely at a picture of a pilot in his mask, and he does indeed look half-pig, half-man. Nostradamus had no idea what these strange creatures were, but his description is brilliant. The 'brute beast' who is 'talking' is a reference to the radio transmission between the various squadrons of British and German fighters as they battle it out over the English countryside.

*"The inhabitants of Marseilles completely changed,
Flight and pursuit right up to the approaches of Lyons.
Narbonne, Toulouse outraged by Bordeaux;
Killed and captive are almost a million."*

Century I Quatrain 72

Above: Visions of German U-boat submarines hunting shipping in the Atlantic in 'wolf packs', puzzled the seer of Salon, who described them as sea-serpents, capable of killing at long distance.

The outraged' towns named by Nostradamus were under the rule of the hated Vichy Government of war-time France. It is estimated that 863,000 French people died in World War II.

"Near the harbours within two cities,
There will happen two scourges the like of
which was never before seen
Famine, pestilence within, people put out by
the sword.
They cry for help from the great
immortal God!"

Century II Quatrain 6

This is an unmistakable reference to the atomic blasts that ended the war. The 'two cities' are, of course, Hiroshima and Nagasaki, which were both devastated by atomic bombs in two separate attacks in August 1945. In this quatrain, Nostradamus sees the pain and terror of the Japanese as their cities were wiped from the map.

"Shortly afterwards, not a very long interval
A great roaring storm will be raised by land
and sea,
The naval battles will be greater than ever;
Fires, creatures which shoot making
more tumult."

Century II Quatrain 4

The 'great roaring storm' is of course World War II, when naval battles were on an unprecedented scale. The 'creatures that shoot' may well be submarines. It is easy to see how from a 16th-century perspective these sleek, swift craft would resemble sea-serpents.

"In the islands shall be such horrible tumult,
That nothing shall be heard except a warlike
surprise.
So great shall be the attack of the raiders,
That everyone shall shelter himself under the
great line."

Century II Quatrain 100

Here, we have an amazingly accurate account of the Blitz, the nightly bombing raids on London early in the war. Much of the population took refuge every night in the stations of the underground railway system.

"When the great one carries off the prize of
Nuremberg,
Of the Augsburgs, and those of Basel;
Frankfurt retaken by the leader of Cologne.
He will go through Flanders right into
France."

Century III Quatrain 53

This is a brilliant summation of Hitler's rise to power both in Germany and Europe, beginning with the spectacular Nazi Party rallies at Nuremberg, where Hitler's speeches whipped his followers into a frenzy of resentment and indignation about the defeat in World War I and the treaty that followed it, and urged them to follow him in forging a 'glorious' new future for Germany. It was also at Nuremberg that the laws alienating German-Jews were enacted, the first volley in a vicious war against Jewry that was to end in the ashes of Auschwitz.

Below: Adolf Hitler came to power in 1933, when this picture was taken at a rally in Dortmund. Many of his colleagues are wearing the brown shirts of the SA or storm troopers.

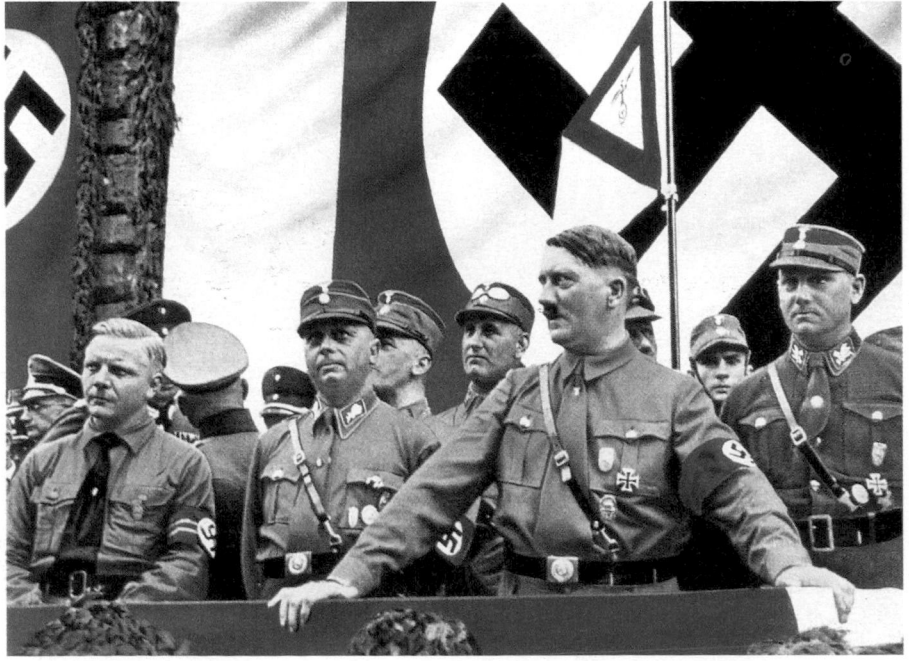

TERROR FROM THE SKIES

The bombing of London was ordered by Hitler in a speech he gave at the Sportspalast in Berlin on 4 September 1940. Ten days earlier, a German Luftwaffe crew had dropped some bombs on the city – not their intended target – when they realized they were lost. Winston Churchill immediately called for a retaliatory strike against Berlin. It did little damage, but gave Hitler his excuse for launching what he called 'total war'. "Mr. Churchill is carrying out these raids not because they promise to be highly effective, but because his air force cannot fly over German soil in daylight. We will stop the handiwork of these night pirates, so help us God! When the British air force drops 3,000 or 4,000 kilograms of bombs, then we will, in one raid, drop 300,000 or 400,000 kilograms. In England they are filled with curiosity and keep asking: 'Why doesn't he come?' Be calm. He is coming! He is coming!"

And come he did, sending wave after wave of bombers in an attempt to destroy the morale of the people of Britain. Londoners took to the Underground to escape the destruction the attacks were causing throughout the city. Unfortunately, not all subway platforms were the safe havens they seemed. When a bomb destroyed water pipes at Balham, 250 people were drowned.

Above and left: The relentless pounding of the Blitz all but destroyed British civilian morale in 1940-41.

Left: Hitler made the immediate militarization of Germany his number one priority straight after he came to power in 1933, thus directly flouting the harsh conditions of the hated Treaty of Versailles, signed after the end of World War I.

Hitler did, of course, send his armies stomping through France in a lightning raid that saw Paris in enemy hands and the British beat a hasty retreat from Dunkirk.

> *"Seven times you will see the British nation change,*
> *Dyed in blood for two hundred and ninety years.*
> *Not at all free though German support,*
> *Aries fears for the protectorage of Poland."*
>
> Century III Quatrain 57

The latter half of the quatrain predicts Britain's determination not to let the Nazi invasion of Poland in September 1939 go unchallenged. It was this act that set off World War II. The first half is somewhat trickier and is open to interpretation. Erika Cheetham believes it could be a reference to Prince Charles. "This may mean that Prince Charles will be the last King on the British throne." Given the recent developments within the House of Windsor, this is not such an outlandish thought. The Royal Family has been wracked by divorce and scandal in recent years, particularly the controversy swirling around Charles and Princess Diana, both of whom readily admitted to committing adultery in television interviews. As the foundations of the monarchy continue to be shaken, there is a growing feeling that Britain might well one day do away with its Royal Family.

alone held out against the might of the Nazi regime. The reference to those outside and dying of starvation has two possible meanings; it is either a reference to the plight of those under the Nazi jackboot in conquered Europe, or to the starvation of the spirit, deprived as it was under the pagan beliefs of Hitler and his henchmen.

"From where he thought to cause famine to come,
From there will come relief supplies.
The eye of the sea watches like a greedy dog,
While one gives the other oil, and wheat."

Century IV Quatrain 35

Hitler tried to starve the British people into submission rather than carry through his grand plans of an armed invasion, after the Luftwaffe lost the Battle of Britain. To this end, he filled the Atlantic with 'wolf packs' of U-boats, which hunted down supply ships containing food stuffs, fuel and vital military equipment coming from America. The 'eye of the sea' is a reference to the submarine periscope.

"The great empire will soon be desolate,
Transformed near the forest of the Ardennes.
The bastards will be beheaded by the oldest,
Aenodard will rule, the hawk-nosed one."

Century V Quatrain 45

Above: Expert Erika Cheetham believes that a quatrain concerning World War II also warns of the imminent collapse of the British monarchy.
Right: Hitler attempted to cripple Britain with regular U-boat attacks on merchant ships crossing the Atlantic with supplies from the USA.

"Those besieged in the islands for a long time
Will take strong measures against their enemies.
Those outside, overcome, will die of hunger,
By such starvation as has never occurred before."

Century III Quatrain 71

This is how Nostradamus depicted the U-boat blockade of Britain during the dark days early in the war while she

The fall of his beloved France in 1940 is foretold in this quatrain. The armies of the Third Reich swept through all resistance on their way to Paris. Amazingly, the thrust of the attack came through the 'forest of the Ardennes'. The 'bastards' might be the two French commanders, Generals Corap and Huntzinger, who blundered in their attempts to stem the Nazi onrush. However, they were not beheaded. Corap was dismissed from the army, while Huntzinger was given the

"The people gathered to see a new spectacle,
Princes and Kings among many onlookers.
Pillars and walls fall, but as if by a miracle
The King and thirty of those present
are saved."

Century VI Quatrain 51

This is an interesting quatrain because it gave rise to Hitler's fascination with the works of Nostradamus. Before the outbreak of war, a Swiss citizen, Ernst Krafft, decided to leave his homeland for Germany, where he hoped his widely-known astrological skills would be of some service to Hitler, whom he greatly admired.

While he was working for Heinrich Himmler, the tyrannical thug who ran the dreaded SS, Krafft warned his superiors in early November 1939, that an assassination attempt would be made on Hitler's life within the next few days. It is believed Kraft used this quatrain to make his prediction. The warning was ignored and forgotten until 8 November, when Hitler gave his yearly address to mark the anniversary of the abortive Nazi coup in Munich in 1923.

Unlike many of his speeches – Hitler loved nothing more than to hear himself talk – this one was cut short because of another matter needing his urgent attention. Less than ten minutes after he and his entourage left the hall, the bomb that had been hidden in a pillar exploded, killing seven and horribly injuring another 63. Krafft knew he had been correct about the forecast, and made sure to mention it to his SS mentors. Initially, they threw him in

NOSTRADAMUS AT WAR

Although Joseph Goebbels had little time for the occult himself, he knew Hitler put great store by it and decided to use Krafft to help in the propaganda war against the allies. Some copies of his interpretations were even found in England. Little attention was paid to them, however, until the fall of France. Following that huge setback, Winston Churchill, by then the Prime Minister, got an interpreter of his own to issue his readings of the prophet's quatrains. After the attack on Pearl Harbor in 1941, the Americans, too, started to heed the words of a Frenchman who had died almost four centuries before!

However, despite the frenzied propaganda attacks his work sparked, Krafft fared poorly in Nazi Germany. When the avowed occultist Rudolph Hess, Hitler's deputy, decided to fly to England in 1941 on a bizarre mission to make peace, Hitler ordered that astrologers and others who dabbled in divining fortunes be routed. Krafft found himself back in prison. He still secretly wrote about the meaning of Nostradamus's predictions for the dreaded Gestapo, which was determined to find anything in the prophet's quatrains that pointed to eventual victory for the Nazis. Alas, the strain of conjuring up such conclusions drove Krafft over the edge, causing him to suffer a nervous breakdown! He never fully recovered, and died an ignominious death, succumbing to typhus while he was being transported to a concentration camp early in 1945.

dishonour of signing the surrender in the very same tram car that had been used to sign the peace of World War I. The 'oldest' as Nostradamus refers to him is General Weygrand, the French commander-in-chief. The hawk-nosed one is no doubt General Charles de Gaulle. The identity of the mysterious 'Aenodard' remains shrouded in mystery, though John Hogue believes it might be a metaphor for one or all three of Nostradamus's Antichrists.

Right: Krafft achieved some eminence within Nazi Germany after using Nostradamus's quatrains to predict an unsuccessful attempt on Hitler's life, but the Führer turned his favour against fortune-tellers after the desertion of Rudolf Hess in 1941.

prison, in the belief that he must have been part of the plot to assassinate Hitler, but shortly afterwards he was freed by Josef Goebbels, the Nazi propaganda chief, and was set to work interpreting Nostradamus's quatrains in a way sympathetic to the Nazis.

Did Nostradamus actually foresee Krafft and his ultimate demise? John Hogue thinks he might have. In Century II, Quatrain 36, Nostradamus wrote:

*"The letters of the great prophet will be seized
And fall into the hands of the tyrant.
His enterprise will be to deceive his king;
But soon his thefts will trouble him."*

*"The royal bird over the city of the Sun
By night will prophesy warnings
For seven months.
The wall of the East will fall."*

Century V Quatrain 81

Interestingly, during the so-called 'phony war', between the declaration and the outbreak of fighting on the western front, German planes dropped pamphlets over Paris – 'the city of the Sun' – that contained Krafft's interpretations of the quatrains that predicted France's defeat.

The 'wall of the East' was the ill-fated Maginot Line, which the Nazis outflanked on their way to Paris. This line has, however, recently led some experts to reinterpret this quatrain as a prediction of the fall of the Berlin Wall, which was certainly erected by those who occupied the area to the east of it.

*"While the eagle is with the cock at Savona,
The Eastern Sea and Hungary will be united.
The army at Naples, Palermo, the marches
of Ancona,
Rome and Venice – a horrible outcry by
the Barb."*

Century VIII Quatrain 89

This describes the last days of the war, when the eagle of America and the cock of France are turning the tide against the Nazis. By 1945, the Soviets

Right: Russian troops raised the red flag on the ruins of the Reichstag – the German parliament building – on 30 April 1945, the day that Hitler took his own life.

had 'liberated' the eastern countries, as well as the vital sea ports on the Black Sea. The Americans were also sweeping through Italy, while the 'Barb' – Hitler – lashed out in a final gasp at the advancing allied armies.

*"A naval engagement will be overcome
by night;
Fire in the ruined ships of the west.
A new code, the great coloured ship,
Anger to the vanquished and victory
in a mist."*

Century IX Quatrain 100

This refers to the Japanese sneak attack on the US naval base at Pearl Harbor, Hawaii, on 7 December 1941. The attack severely damaged the American navy; a large part of its Pacific Fleet was destroyed with little loss to the

enemy. The reference to 'a new code' is believed to refer to the Japanese tactic of using planes launched from aircraft carriers. The same method was used by the Americans with great success in land and sea battles such as Midway, which eventually paved the way for victory over the Japanese empire.

Victory

World War II ended with the Japanese surrender on 2 September 1945, when the Japanese Foreign Minister, Mamoru Shigemitsu, and General Douglas MacArthur formally signed the peace settlement aboard the battleship *USS Missouri*. The greatest tragedy – so far – in the history of mankind, which took the lives of some 55 million people, had come to an end. After signing the declaration, MacArthur, who was visibly

shaking, announced, "It is my earnest hope, indeed the hope of the world, that from this solemn occasion a better world shall emerge out of the blood and carnage of the past."

No one – with the possible exception of Nostradamus – knows if MacArthur's hopes will ever be fulfilled, but war continues to ravage mankind to this day. There has been armed conflict somewhere in the world every day since the end of World War II, and no-one knows when and where the next crisis will break out.

Not so surprisingly, given his reliability in predicting the great calamities of this century and those past, there are many people who believe Nostradamus has the answers to these questions. Indeed, many researchers say he not only saw the Gulf War of 1991,

but also the great battles to come in World War III.

"He will enter, wicked, unpleasant, infamous,
Tyrannizing over Mespotamia.
All friends made by the adulterous lady,
The land dreadful and black in aspect."

Century VIII Quatrain 70

In this quatrain, Nostradamus foresaw Operation Desert Storm, when an alliance of most of the western nations of the world drew a line in the sand and dared Iraqi despot Saddam Hussein to cross it. The area

Below and right: The bombing of Pearl Harbour on 7 December 1941 left the powerful American Pacific Fleet in ruins, but the outrage served to bring the United States officially into the war as a significant power on the side of the allies.

quatrains, America will eventually triumph in the coming conflict.

"At sunrise a great fire will be seen,
Noise and light extending to the north.
Within the globe death and cries are heard,
Death awaiting them through weapons, fire
and famine."

Century II Quatrain 91

The renowned Nostradamus expert Erika Cheetham believes this quatrain is an ominous foretelling of a war between the Americans and Russians. In view of the lessening tensions between the

Above and right: Nostradamus foresaw the devastation of the Gulf War, when the invading Iraqis were driven from Kuwait by combined Western and Arab forces; as they retreated they set fire to many of the oil fields, leaving 'the land dreadful and black in aspect'.

Nostradamus knew as Mespotamia is modern-day Iraq and Kuwait. In 1990, Hussein sent his army across the border into Kuwait to take over the vast oil fields of his country's tiny, though immensely wealthy neighbour. After he was driven back to Baghdad by the allies, he ordered the oil wells be set on fire, leaving "the land dreadful and black in aspect'. However, John Hogue suggests in *Nostradamus: The New Revelations* that there might be more to this quatrain than at first meets the eye. "How a prophecy is interpreted often depends on the prejudices of the interpreter. To most Iraqis, especially those digging out from numerous US Cruise missile attacks, and to many poor and down-trodden Arabs in the Middle East, the greater "tyrant" is President George Bush, or even Bill Clinton."

Future Wars

As for the futuristic apocalypse of World War III, Nostradamus paints a terrifying portrait of nuclear holocaust and widespread death and destruction. It is clear it will start in 1999 – if man does not change his ways. Some quatrains appear to point to a huge war between the USA and Russia, while others suggest

it will arise out of tensions caused by the third Antichrist – whom we shall deal with in detail in the next chapter – somewhere in the Middle East.

"The gods will make it seem to mankind
That they are the authors of a great war.
Before the sky was seen to be free of weapons
and rockets:
The greatest damage will be afflicted towards
the left side."

Century I Quatrain 91

This quatrain on World War III talks clearly of rockets being launched against the opposing forces. Traditionally, America is placed on the left hand side of a map of the world, indicating it could suffer great losses in the coming conflagration. But as he notes in other

world's two great superpowers, this might seem an unlikely scenario. But just because the Berlin Wall is down and Moscow and Washington are not currently at each other's throats does not mean some future spark could not reignite hostilities. To be sure, in Russia today there are hardline leaders who have vowed to rebuild the Soviet empire, which would surely bring an American response. There are also rebel forces inside the former Soviet Union who have threatened to steal or develop a nuclear weapon and use it to get their demands.

In one of his most horrifying quatrains dealing with World War III, Nostradamus sees the destruction of New York, one of the world's most populous cities.

Above: The modern inter-continental ballistic missile can carry hugely destructive nuclear warheads a third of the way around the world.

Left: The destruction of Hiroshima by atomic bomb is, according to Nostradamus, a pale shadow of what is to come during World War III.

Below: The evidence that New York is the 'New City' to be destroyed by fire is flimsy. The 45° mentioned in the quatrain is much more likely to be the elevation of an astrological event than a line of latitude.

"The sky will burn at forty-five degrees,
Fire approaches the great New City.
Immediately a huge, scattered flame leaps up
When they want to have proof of the
Normans."

Century VI Quatrain 97

The 'great New City' is regarded by most to be New York. New York County lies between 40° and 45° of latitude. However, there are other interpretations of this quatrain. One of the latest suggests that the city is not New York but New Belgrade, a suburb of the Serbian capital, which is situated at 45° latitude.

"The new empire in desolation will be
changed
From the Northern pole. From Sicily
Will come such trouble that it will
Bother the enterprise tributary to Philip."

Century VIII Quatrain 81

This quatrain speaks of a civilization moving southwards, possibly after a nuclear holocaust, as survivors look for new lands and food sources left uncontaminated by atomic fallout. The references to Sicily and Philip could mean the war will begin on the Italian island or Spain. Nostradamus makes some mention of a future Moslem invasion of the Mediterranean, particularly in Italy, indicating the holocaust could be triggered by this.

CHAPTER FIVE

The Third Antichrist

Who will come next?

◆

Even those with just a passing interest in Nostradamus know he spoke of three antichrists - disciples of evil who would wreak terrible havoc on an unsuspecting world. The first two were Napoleon Bonaparte and Adolf Hitler, undeniably power-crazed dictators who thought nothing of killing untold numbers to solidify their rule. But in this chapter, we will also take a new look at the mysterious third antichrist, the one which recent research indicates could be among us even today.

Sometimes referred to as Mabus - though Erika Cheetham, author of *The Prophecies of Nostradamus* thinks Mabus may only be a forerunner - the final antichrist may not be a world figure like his predecessors. Indeed, it is only in very modern times that scholars have come to believe Mabus might be an obscure terrorist, who lights the fuse of a great holocaust. Similarly, the latest thinking is that he could actually steal a nuclear weapon...something many terrorists are right now trying to obtain. The freshest interpretations indicate that he could find help from the Communist Chinese.

Left: Although he made administrative reforms and was at times brilliant in battle, Napoleon's cynicism, arrogance and irreligiousness made him an Antichrist in Nostradamus's eyes.

deaths of more than 50 million people, the majority of them civilians far removed from the scene of battle.

What, then, of the third Antichrist, the one that Nostradamus predicts will deliver Hell on Earth? Before we scan the quatrains searching for our answer – an answer many readers will be chilled to learn is fast approaching – we must first look back at his predictions concerning Napoleon and Hitler, because if he were right about them, could he not also be right about the man he called 'Mabus', the third and last Antichrist, already said to be among us?

The Little Emperor

Nostradamus devoted a slew of quatrains to Napoleon Bonaparte, which is not altogether surprising since the prophet took a particularly keen interest in the affairs of his native land. The first mention of Napoleon comes in Century I Quatrain 76.

"A man will be called by a ferocious name,
That the three sisters will have his name
for destiny.
He will speak then to a great people in
words and deeds.
More than any other man he will have fame
and renown."

From his cramped study overlooking the peaceful countryside of Provence, Nostradamus saw evil that knew no bounds. Plagues and catastrophes,as well as devastating wars, filled his visions, and he was sometimes all but overcome by the constant smell of death down through the ages. But of all the stark horrors that he saw, nothing filled him with as much dread as his gruesome visions of the three men he referred to as the Antichrists.

To Nostradamus – and indeed many others who have studied the quatrains – they epitomized demonic horror, vicious brutes who would lead their nations into cataclysmic struggles against their neighbours. The rise to power and infamous actions of these three man-

beasts is a constant theme in the great prophet's works, as he coolly details their crimes against humanity and the despair they wrought.

As we have seen in earlier chapters, the first two Antichrists have been identified as Napoleon Bonaparte, whose war to unify Europe under the French flag cost more than two million people their lives, and Adolf Hitler, the Austrian-born despot who unleashed all the terrors of World War II, including the so-called 'Final Solution', and was thus to some degree responsible for the

Right: Only a few right-wing cranks would argue with the conclusion that Adolf Hitler, the second Antichrist, was one of the most vile and destructive men who ever lived.

Ein Volk, ein Reich, ein Führer!

The latest research has revealed that the 'ferocious name' is the Greek word for destroyer, *appolyon*. The name is familiar to students of the Bible. *Revelations* 9.11 refers to "The angel of abyss, whose name, in Hebrew, is Abbadon, and in Greek, Appolyon, the Destroyer". Experts believe Appolyon is Napoleon. The three sisters of the quatrain could be Napoleon's real-life kin, Elisa, Caroline and Pauline, or the three Fates of Greek mythology.

Nostradamus makes a second reference to Napoleon as the first Antichrist in the first quatrain of Century VIII: "Pau, Nay, Loron will be more of fire than of the blood." John Hogue believes this is an abstruse cypher. "Pau Nay Loron swivelled once becomes Nay Pau Loron, and twice Napaulon Roy = Napoleon the King. The spelling for Napoleon in Corsican style is even closer to the anagram, Napauleone." Of course, Hogue may be stretching ingenuity too far.

> *"Of a name that never belonged to a Gallic king,*
> *Never was there so terrible a thunderbolt.*
> *He made Italy tremble, Spain and the English.*
> *He wooed a foreign lady with assiduity."*
>
> Century IV Quatrain 54

This quatrain barely needs explanation. Napoleon Bonaparte was not of royal blood, and no French king ever bore the name. And he did indeed strike across Europe like a horrible thunderbolt, instilling terror into the hearts of freedom-loving men everywhere. The last line may be a reference to his second wife, Marie-Louise of Austria, whom he treated shabbily, or perhaps to the Empress Josephine, who, though French, was born on the West Indian island of Martinique. It could also refer to one of his many affairs.

> *"From a simple soldier he will rise to the empire,*
> *From the short robe he will attain the long.*
> *Able in arms, in church government he shows less skill;*
> *He raises or depresses the priests as water a sponge."*
>
> Century VIII Quatrain 57

Napoleon was a common – though extremely gifted – soldier until his phenomenal rise to total power, first as consul and then emperor. When he was appointed consul for life in 1799, he changed the familiar consular tunic for a longer robe. Without doubt, as Nostradamus also predicts, Napoleon exasperated the church of Rome for much of his reign.

> *"Ready to fight he will desert,*
> *The chief adversary will be victorious*
> *The rear guard will make a defence,*
> *Those who falter dying in the white country."*
>
> Century IV Quatrain 75

Nostradamus foresees the debacle of Napoleon's ruinous Russian campaign of 1812. The French forces made it to Moscow, but the remaining population of the largely-abandoned capital put it to the torch rather than let their enemies lay claim to it. Moscow was ablaze for several days, and after the fires died down, Napoleon realized he had to withdraw and return across the icy wastelands of Russia to France. Tragically for his army, Napoleon abandoned them to their own devices, fleeing back to Paris in disguise in order to avoid the bands of marauding

UNHEEDED REVELATIONS

Napoleon, like the Antichrist who would follow him to power more than 130 years later, was a dark, solitary figure ill at ease in company and a man who had few intimates. In fact, historians say only Josephine Beauharnais ever got really close to him, as did Eva Braun with Adolf Hitler. Unlike Braun, who was an uncomplicated country girl, Josephine was a sophisticated, well-read woman who, ironically, was very familiar with the writings of Nostradamus, as the aristocracy of Europe has long been. Maybe Napoleon should have listened to her more closely, because history records that she was firmly against his ill-founded plans to invade Russia, fearing the great prophet's dire forecast of a terrible defeat. The Emperor ignored her entreaties, and forged ahead with his massive assault against Moscow, with disastrous consequences for himself and France. In World War II, Hitler made the same mistake, and saw his vision of world conquest come to an ignominious end on the frozen steppes of the Soviet Union as the Communists turned back the tide of Operation Barbarossa.

Above: Contrary to Messonier's romanticized painting, there was nothing dignified or noble about Napoleon's precipitate retreat from Moscow, which resulted in the destruction of his Great Army.

Cossacks that attacked and harried the French as they beat a humiliating retreat home through a fierce winter. Many men died in the skirmishes with the hardy Cossacks, but far more perished from the cold, hunger and disease. In all, just 20,000 men returned out of an original force some half a million strong. Like Hitler, Napoleon placed little value on the lives of his men.

"A mass of men will draw near coming from Slavonia.
The Destroyer will ruin the old city.
He will see his Romania quite deserted,
Then will not know how to extinguish the great flame."

Century IV Quatrain 82

Here is an overview of Napoleon's changing fortunes. The Destroyer devastates the old city (Moscow), but after that initial triumph, there is only

disaster. His infant son, Napoleon II, had only recently been made King of Rome – or Romania as Nostradamus calls it – but Napoleonic power there evaporated as his demise approached. The 'great flame' is probably a reference to the wars that Napoleon started, and which eventually consumed him and France.

"The vanquished prince is exiled in Italy,
Escaped by sea sailing past Genoa and Marseilles.
He is then crushed by a massive concentration of foreign armies.
Though he escapes the fire the bees will drained to extinction."

Century X Quatrain 24

After fleeing exile on the isle of Elba, Napoleon landed in the southern part of France, near the ancient city of Marseilles. Here, he rallied loyal troops for what would turn out to be his last

Above: Even in exile, Napoleon did not abandon his dreams of glory, plotting escape while he dictated his memoirs to his aides.

Left: Napoleon's desire for an heir led him to divorce Josephine and marry the Austrian arch-duchess Marie-Louise. Napoleon II was born in 1811, but died at the age of 21.

campaign, which ended when the combined armies of Britain and Prussia routed his forces at Waterloo. The 'bees drained to extinction' refers to Napoleon's personal emblem.

"The great empire will soon be exchanged for a small place,
Which will soon begin to grow.
A very small place of tiny area in the middle of which
He will come to lay down his sceptre."

Century I Quatrain 32

Nostradamus never referred to France as an empire until after Napoleons's rise, so there is no doubt he is speaking of the conqueror here. Even more proof is offered by the theme of the quatrain, dealing with Napoleon's exile from France, first to Elba then later to St Helena. As Nostradamus predicted, the empire was exchanged for a small place (Elba), then began to grow once Napoleon escaped and began his plans of conquest all over again. After just 100 days of freedom, he was recaptured and eventually banished to St Helena – an

The seer called him Hister, a name that has beguiled Nostradamus researchers since Hitler began his rise to power. Before that, interpreters believed that Nostradamus used Hister to mean the River Danube, known by that name in Roman times. The modern theory is that Nostradamus used the word to combine the Nazi leader's name with his birthplace: Hitler grew up in Linz, close by the Danube.

"Beasts wild with hunger will cross the rivers
The greater part of the battlefield will be
against Hister.
He will drag the leader in a cage of iron,
Where the child of Germany observes
no law."

Century II Quatrain 24

even smaller island – where he was finally forced to relinquish his hold on power, here symbolized by a sceptre.

"The general who led infinite hosts
Will end his life far from where he was born.
Among five thousand people of strange
custom
Upon a chalk island in the sea."

Century I Quatrain 98

Death indeed did come to Napoleon far from his beloved France, on the island of St Helena, among strangers whose ways and customs were alien to him. Just as he had mapped out Napoleon's life and conquests with amazing accuracy, Nostradamus also successfully foretold his death. The world had survived the first Antichrist, who, despite his depradations, did many positive things for his country; his Code is still the basis for French law, for instance. However, a much more evil one was to rise in Germany, and bring the world to the brink of destruction.

The Second Antichrist

Adolf Hitler, currently the most hated and reviled man in history, was born in the Austrian town of Braunau in 1889, the son of a domineering father and a doting mother. In an epistle to one of his books, Nostradamus wrote that during the years '37 to '45, "An infernal power will rise against the Church of Jesus Christ. This shall be the second Antichrist."

Above: Hitler's involvement with the occult remains debatable, but his modern admirers, several of them psychopathic serial killers, have shown an acquaintance with Satanic symbols.

Below: Even with the benefit of hindsight, Hitler's horoscope does not show outstanding evil.

The German who observed no law is of course Hitler, who let loose his 'beasts wild with hunger' across the boundaries of Europe and the Soviet Union. The reference to dragging leaders in a cage of iron could be a reference to the medieval practice of humiliating defeated enemy

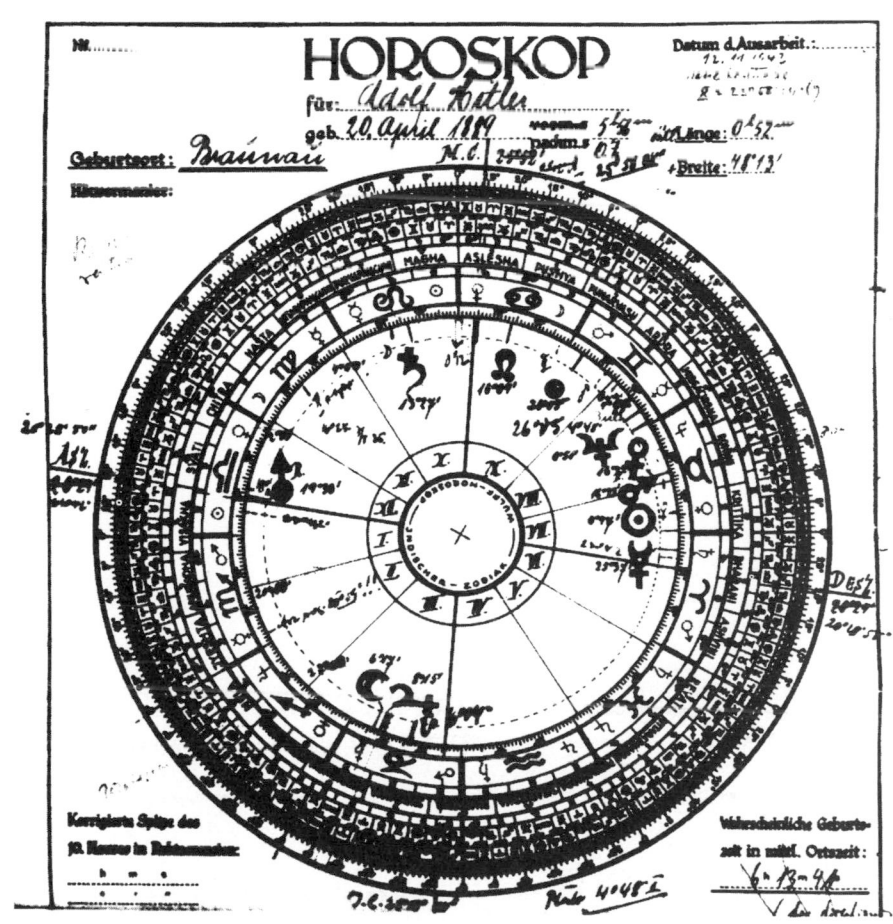

THE STRUGGLE FOR POWER

Adolf Hitler arrived in Munich a nondescript, impoverished artist, early in 1919. A decorated veteran of World War I, he swiftly immersed himself in the political intrigue and upheaval of the city, and joined the right-wing German Workers Party. He quickly came to lead this extremely nationalistic cluster of misfits through his uncanny ability to organize and his persuasive oratory. He soon took the party even further to the right, renaming it the National Socialist German Workers Party (*Nationalsozialistiche Deutsche Arbeiterspartei*, or Nazi for shot) and adopting the crooked cross, or swastika, as its emblem. He also recruited brutish army veterans to his own private brown-shirted army, the Storm Troopers, who put down hecklers at meetings and fought in the streets with political opponents. Once firmly in control, he set about defining the party's goals: the rescinding of the Treaty of Versailles,which had ended World War I; a profit sharing plan in industry; the confiscation of all war profits; and the ostracization of German Jews.

In 1923, as inflation ripped through the war-damaged economy of the Weimar Republic, he launched a coup, or *putsch*, in a meeting in a large Munich beer hall. Surrounded by Storm Troopers, he stunned the assembly by declaring, "The national revolution has begun." It was an ill-timed pronouncement; the following day Hitler was arrested. He was sentenced to five years imprisonment in Landsberg Fortress, but served just nine months, during which time he worked on *Mein Kampf* ("My Struggle"), an ugly, ill-written and unwieldy tome in which he set out his plans for

Germany's – and Europe's – future. The book would become the 'Bible' of the National Socialist Party.

After his release, Hitler decided to obtain power through the ballot box – though the Storm Troopers were rarely able to resist a little electoral intimidation – and had greater and greater success as the increasingly fed-up German people began turning to him as their saviour from the burdens of Versailles and the rabble-rousing Communists. Following an election early in 1933, in which the Nazis won 288 of 608 seats in the federal Reichstag, Hitler proclaimed victory. Within weeks, he had assumed total power in Germany, outlawing all other political parties and ordering most of his opponents into exile or prison.

He also made sure that no-one within the party would grow powerful enough to challenge his supreme authority by ordering the murders of former loyalists in the 'Night of the Long Knives'. About a hundred Nazis were purged. Among his victims were Ernst Rohm, the head of the Storm Troopers, who was executed by members of Hitler's elite force, the SS. Following Rohm's death, the brown shirts were disbanded. In the following six years Hitler turned Germany into the most efficient and ruthless military power on the face of the Earth.

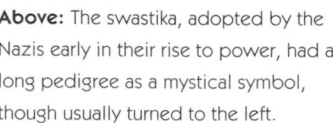

Above: The swastika, adopted by the Nazis early in their rise to power, had a long pedigree as a mystical symbol, though usually turned to the left.

Left: Hitler presided over a party that preached purity but was led by a motley collection of madmen, mystics, sadists and opportunists.

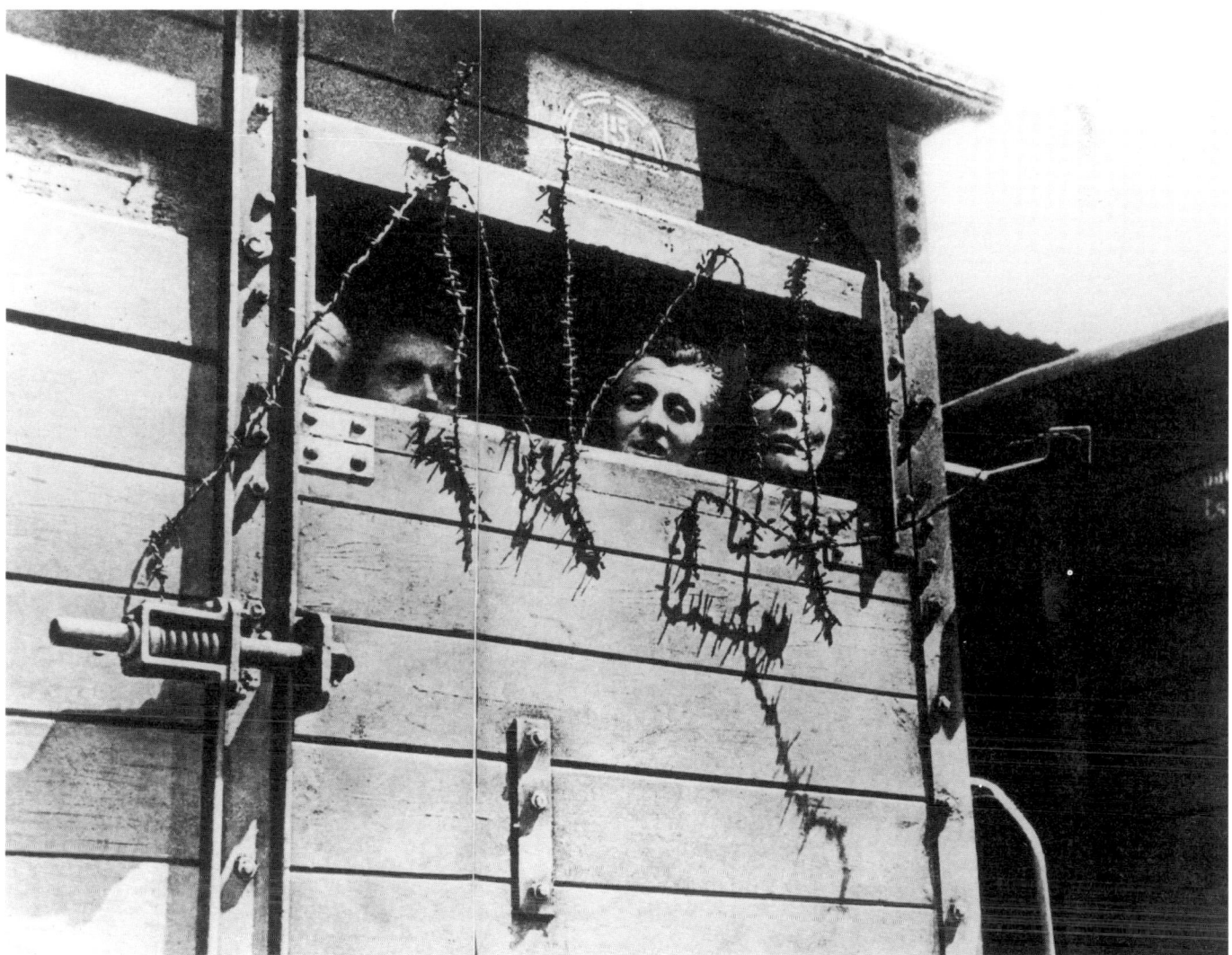

chiefs by caging them and displaying them in public squares. There is no doubt that Hitler took pleasure in humiliating his enemies by raising the swastika over their homelands or, as he did with the French, by insisting they sign the surrender in the very same tram car used for the formal German surrender after World War I. Some new researchers believe this could also be a reference to Mussolini, whose body was strung up by Italian partisans from the steel frame of a burned-out petrol station.

"A leader of Great Germanies will come to give help which is only counterfeit.
He will stretch the borders of Germany, and cause France to be divided into two.
Living fire and death hidden in globes will be loosed,
Horrible and terrible, by night the enemy will reduce cities to dust."

Century IX Quatrain 90

If anyone else fits the description in this quatrain more closely than Hitler, civilization certainly has yet to hear from him. It is an amazingly clear prediction. Hitler indeed built a greater Germany – which he called 'Grossdeutschland' – in the years immediately before the outbreak of war. On 7 March 1936, he ordered his troops across the Rhine, retaking the territory of the Rhineland, which had been demilitarized by the Treaty of Versailles as a buffer zone between France and Germany.

New Order

On 12 March 1938, Hitler fused Germany and Austria in the Anschlüss pact, harshly suppressing any resistance to his 'new order'. Communists and socialists were whipped and beaten in the streets and Jews were forced to scrub the streets and public lavatories of Vienna. A few months later, in October,

Above: Once the war was in progress, there was no impediment to the implementation of the Final Solution. 'Undesirables' were shipped to their deaths in convoys of cattle trucks.

the western powers appeased Hitler by allowing him to take possession of the Sudetenland in Czechoslovakia. Greater Germany was now complete – and war was imminent. This stunningly accurate quatrain goes further, peering into the fall of France. After the peace agreement of 22 June 1940, France was indeed carved into two parts, while Nostradamus's description of the globes carrying fire and death is an obvious reference to the night bombing which reduced parts of many allied – and later German – cities to blazing rubble. This is one of Nostradamus's most accurate – and terrifyingly vivid – visions.

Nostradamus also saw the Hell of Hitler's 'final solution' to the 'Jewish

THE FINAL SOLUTION

More than six million Jews, as well as other peoples the Nazis called *untermensch* or sub-humans – gypsies, Slavs, homosexuals, the mentally handicapped, and so on – perished in the death camps. Most of them were killed by poison gas developed in the chemical factories of Germany. The Holocaust, which has become a watershed in the history of man, began in 1941, following eight years of increasingly repressive actions against the Jews of Europe, who were systematically beaten, shot and clubbed to death by the jackbooted thugs of the SS. Following the invasion of Russia, the mass killings began in earnest, when Nazi death squads followed the advancing armies killing Jews and others wherever they could be found. In the ensuing months, the bloodshed grew worse, as literally hundreds of thousands of *untermensch* were dragged from their homes by Nazis and Ukrainian volunteers and slaughtered with machine-gun fire in remote forests and fields.

Then, following the Wannsee Conference of 20 January 1942, a more diabolical plan was put into practice. At this meeting, in a grand old house in a genteel suburb of Berlin, Dante's *Inferno* came to life, under the watchful eye of Reinhard Heydrich, the head of the SS Intelligence Service. Together, he and his fellow butchers – among them the infamous 'grand architect' of the Holocaust, Adolf Eichmann – set about organizing the mass shipment of Jews and other 'undesirables' to the horror of the concentration camps.

It was, in fact, no great secret that a dire fate awaited Jews under the Nazis, though the actual details remained a mystery until the end of the war. Hitler had, after all, suggested the total destruction of European Jewry in his sordid diatribe, *Mein*

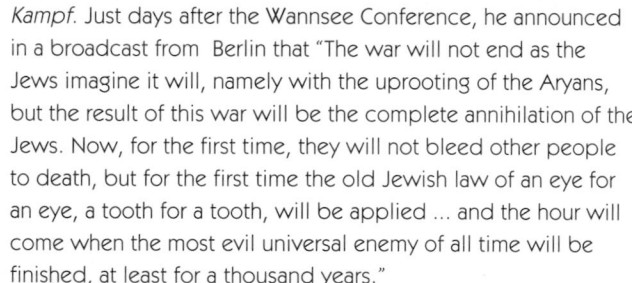

Kampf. Just days after the Wannsee Conference, he announced in a broadcast from Berlin that "The war will not end as the Jews imagine it will, namely with the uprooting of the Aryans, but the result of this war will be the complete annihilation of the Jews. Now, for the first time, they will not bleed other people to death, but for the first time the old Jewish law of an eye for an eye, a tooth for a tooth, will be applied ... and the hour will come when the most evil universal enemy of all time will be finished, at least for a thousand years."

Hitler almost made good on his abominable threat, as the Jews of Europe were herded into the camps to face unspeakable brutalities, sadistic medical experiments and ultimately death. After the liberation, the few pathetic survivors of Hitler's madness were found wandering the camps by the advancing allied armies. Even veteran soldiers, such as the American generals Dwight D Eisenhower and George 'Blood and Guts' Patton, were sickened by what they saw. An American congressman, on an inspection tour of the camps after the war, claimed that "If you tried to tell the actual facts, you'd get into filth and obscenity that would be unprintable." German citizens who lived near the camps were forced by the allied armies to

visit the hell holes in their back yards. Many claimed they were totally unaware of the atrocities committed under their very noses, but reporters and other officials sneered at that excuse. As one journalist eloquently put it, "They collapsed of hunger at their benches, and no-one asked why. They died along the road on the long walk to camp, and no-one expressed surprise. The good citizens shut their eyes and their ears and their nostrils to the sight and sound and smell of this place."

As the Nazis moved through Europe, streams of refugees fled before them (left), but for many there was no escape. The implementation of the Final Solution was entrusted to Hitler's elite force, the SS (above), who organized and ran the death camps such as Auschwitz (above right). Inmates were gassed and their bodies burned in incinerators (right) that never went cold.

question'. In an introduction to one of his Centuries, he warns:

"The shocking and infamous one will bring fear of the great furnace.
First the chosen one, the captives not returning:
The world's lowest crime, the Angry Female 'Irale' not at ease,
Barb, Hister, Malta. And the Empty one does not return."

The 'infamous one' is of course Hitler, who consigned to the great furnaces of Auschwitz and other death camps millions of Jews – or 'chosen ones' – in what we now refer to as the Holocaust, surely the most cruel and dastardly crime ever perpetrated by man against man. The "Angry Female 'Irale'" could be a reference to Israel, which even today does battle with Hitler's anti-Semitic legacy. However, Nostradamus

could well perish unless he is thwarted.

Clues to his identity and his arrival can be found in the quatrains, though experts disagree over the actual role he will play in the great war to come. He could well be another Napoleon or Hitler, who commands great armies, but some modern scholars of the prophet's

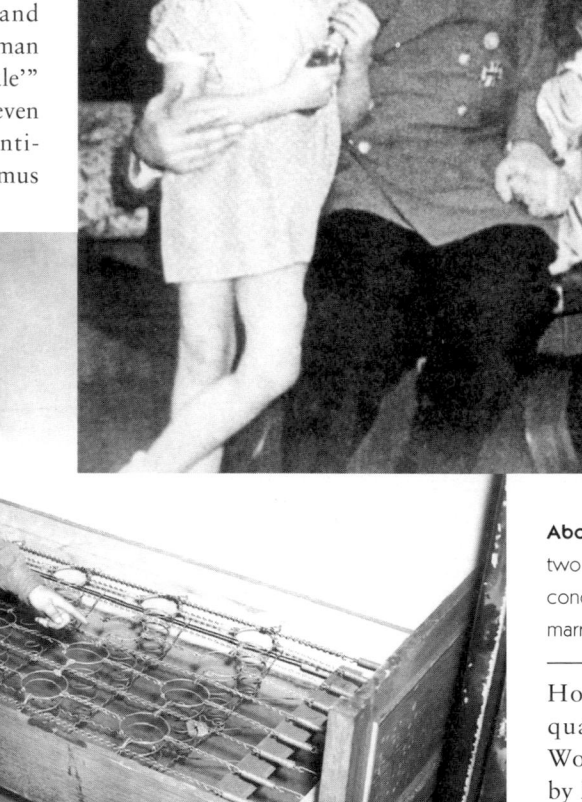

Above and left: Hitler and Eva Braun (seen with two unknown children) spent their last days in a concrete bunker in Berlin. On 30 April 1945 they married and committed suicide there.

Mabus will spring from the Middle East or Northern Africa, because he mentions 'Baal', a name given to various gods worshipped in the area in ancient times, particularly in the Phoenecian empire. At its height, Phoenecia encompassed modern nations like Syria, Lebanon, Iraq, Israel, Libya, Palestine and Tunisia.

However, in his most remarkable quatrain regarding the beginning of World War III – which will be sparked by Mabus – Nostradamus sees a 'King of Terror' come among us, and gives the exact date we can expect the holocaust.

"In the year 1999 and seven months
The great King of Terror will come from the sky
He will bring back Genghis Khan
Before and after Mars rules happily."

Century X Quatrain 72

also sees ultimate victory over the forces of darkness, declaring that the empty or soulless one (Hitler) shall not return.

Nostradamus researchers all agree that there is no positive identification for 'Mabus', the third great monster who will again plunge the world into a catastrophic war. All we know for certain is that he will not come from Europe, that he will spark World War III, and, most ominously, that mankind

works suggest he might an obscure terrorist or factional leader who sets off the all-consuming conflict with a strategically-placed nuclear weapon or an assassination.

Indeed, Erika Cheetham now believes that Mabus may not be the dreaded third Antichrist: "I think it is more likely that he is envisaged as a forerunner, so the time of the Antichrist is still awaited." Nostradamus gives clues that

There is little doubt that Nostradamus saw the beginning of the war as July, 1999, when the hideous king of terror – either the Antichrist himself or his weapons –

will come from the sky. Could it be a reference to intercontinental ballistic missiles, or, as some modern scholars suggest, a reference to the hijacking of an aeroplane, an event commonly used by terrorists to spread fear? He also says Mars, the Roman god of war, will rule happily. But what of the third line and the reference to Genghis Khan? Could it simply be a reminder to us that the scourge will be like that of the great Mongol Khan and his Golden Horde – the so-called Devil's Horsemen – who swept through Asia and much of Eastern Europe hundreds of years earlier. Or is this another clue to the identity of the third Antichrist?

The latest studies believe that Nostradamus may have been hinting that Mabus – and remember he may not be anyone we will ever remember – may find support from the East, in China, through another 'Roi d'Angolmois' or Mongol king. To be sure, Mongolia itself is not a major player on the world

Above: To Nostradamus, a 16th-century Catholic, an Antichrist was a Devil, or Satan incarnate.
Below: Several interpreters feel the third antichrist will be a follower of Islam, whose holy book, the *Koran*, abjures followers to defend their faith.

stage, but there is evidence that China is moving closer to some of the more dangerous leaders in the Middle East, and has already helped Iran and Libya with the materiel needed to create a nuclear capability.

As the West continues to isolate Beijing in the wake of the Tiananmen Square massacre, it might be that China and fundamentalist Moslems will forge an open alliance against the European and American democracies.

There are other clues in the quatrains that might link the third Antichrist to China, or at least the Orient.

*"From the three water signs will be
born a man
Who will celebrate Thursday as his feast day.
His renown, praise, rule and power will grow
By land and sea, bringing trouble to the east."*

Century I Quatrain 50

The only drawback here is that no great religion – certainly not Islam – celebrates Thursday as a holy day of the week.

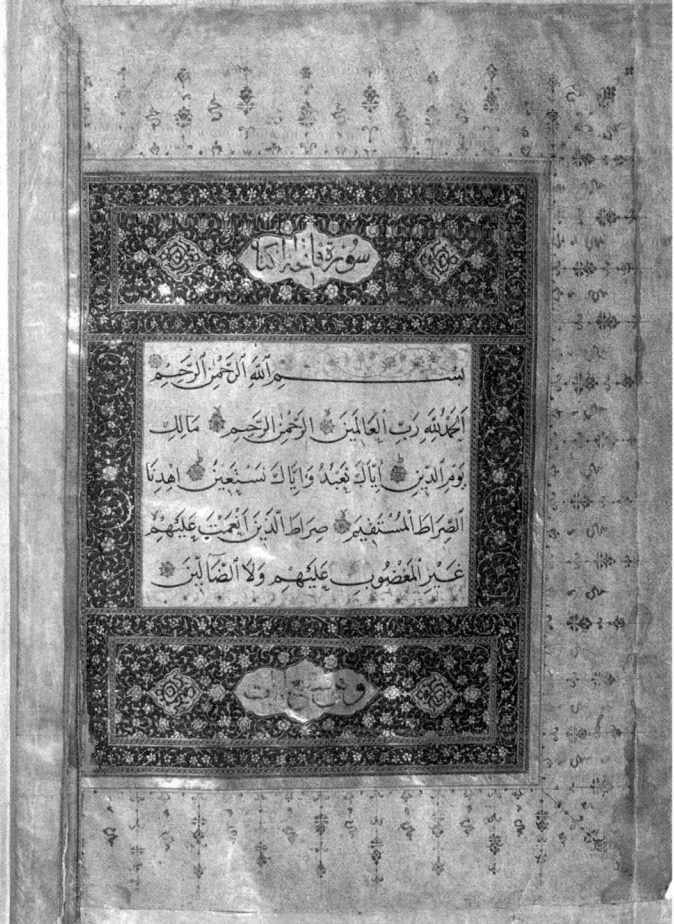

Above: Many commentators fear that Mabus may be a terrorist or renegade ruler who uses missiles – probably made and sold in the West – to launch an attack that triggers World War III.

The eastern origins of the third Antichrist are also prefigured in the lines of Century II, Quatrain 29.

"The Eastern man will come forth from
his seat
And will cross the Apennines to France.
His will cross through the sky, the seas and
the snows
And he will strike everyone with his rod."

There seems, however, to be on balance more evidence in the quatrains to support the widespread belief that the third Antichrist will come from the Middle East than there is that he will rise from deeper in Asia.

Nostradamus makes the first of several references to the mysterious Mabus in Century II, Quatrain 62.

"Mabus will soon die, then will come
A horrible slaughter of people and animals.
At once vengeance is revealed coming from a
hundred hands.
Thirst and famine when the comet will pass."

There are several things to look for in this quatrain. The last line certainly refers to Halley's Comet, which tells us that Mabus was among us at the time of its most recent reappearance, in 1985 to 1986. This could mean that whatever seed was to spark World War III might have been sewn ten years ago, and that we are starting to reap the consequences in famine and drought, both of which are now widespread in many nations. Even developed countries like America and Australia have experienced devastating droughts in recent years.

This quatrain also tells us that Mabus will not be around for long – he may indeed already be dead – giving further credence to the newer thinking that the

THE MIGHTY KHAN

Genghis Khan, or Temujin, was a butcher whose cruelty knew no bounds as his hordes rampaged through Asia, the Mid-East and eastern Europe in the 13th Century. "The greatest pleasure," he once remarked, "is to vanquish your enemies and chase them before you, to rob them of their wealth and see those dear to them bathed in tears, to ride their horses and clasp to their bosom their wives and daughters."

From humble beginnings on the plains of what we now call Mongolia, he rose to be a powerful warrior within his tribe, who, by force of arms, eventually forged a federation with the other clans who inhabited the area. Once united, the Mongols became a force unlike any seen before in history. In vast numbers, they poured out of their cold, wind-swept home across Asia and China, south to the Islamic world then into Europe, conquering all before them with their lightning-quick raids. To those who lived during the time of the Mongols, there was no more gut-churning sight than seeing these ferocious warriors charge into battle on their speedy horses.

last Antichrist will not necessarily be a leader, but a terrorist or assassin. John Hogue has an interesting theory on the possible origins of Mabus. He notes that before it was given access to once-occupied territories, the headquarters of the Palestine Liberation Organisation were located just a few miles from the ruins of the ancient Carthaginian town of Thurbo Majus in Tunisia. Could Nostradamus have mistaken Mabus for Majus? The 'hundred hands' of vengeance could be a reference to the many factions within the PLO, or to the numerous refugee camps where disgruntled Palestinians have spent so many years in recent times.

Yet there are other clues which would seem to point away from the PLO as the spawning ground of the Antichrist.

"One who the infernal Gods of Hannibal
Will cause to be born, terror to all mankind;
Never more horror nor the newspapers tell of
worse in the past,
Then will come to the Italians through
Babel."

Century II Quatrain 30

Nostradamus's Babel is modern-day Iraq, where the despotic Saddam Hussein still rules with an iron fist despite the wholesale rout of his forces in the Gulf War. As we know from recent accounts, Hussein continues to defy the civilized world by stubbornly pressing ahead with his dream of one day owning a weapon of mass destruction – either nuclear, biological or chemical – despite tight sanctions by the United Nations.

First Strike

Nostradamus suggests that the lords of terror will strike at the West first in Italy. Whether this means an actual attack on the country itself – or on religions in general – is open to debate. Astonishingly, the fact that Nostradamus makes mention of newspapers in this quatrain is almost overlooked when one considers the grave totality in this passage. There were no newspapers in the prophet's day!

Some scholars believe this quatrain does refer to Saddam Hussein. They feel the key is in the first line, in which Nostradamus speaks of 'the infernal Gods of Hannibal'. Hannibal was a Carthaginian, so they claim the prophet was referring to North Africa, perhaps to Libya, whose leader, Moammar Gaddafi, is no friend of the western democracies.

If not Saddam or the PLO, could it be another monster currently among us who gives rise to the war? Let's look at another amazing passage which seems to point a finger at someone else. And remember, Mabus does not have to be a king or president or even a politician, even though his hand is surely on the torch that will ignite World War III. In Century III, Quatrain 60 Nostradamus talks of blood flowing because of the actions of 'a dark man who is filled with evil' whose support comes from Iran and Iraq.

"Throughout Asia there will be great
proscription,
Also in Mysia, Lycia and Pamphalia.
Blood will flow because of a dark man,
Who is filled with evil."

Prior to 1985, people in the west thought that the *nom de guerre* Abu Nidal – taken by the infamous Arab terrorist Sabri al-Banna – meant 'Father of Struggle', but in a revealing interview that year, Nidal redefined his name to mean 'Father of Evil'. He referred to himself as an 'evil spirit' and considered himself more dangerous to western democracy than an atomic bomb. Note that the year he gave the interview was the same year Halley's Comet made its most recent reappearance.

Recent studies offer a fascinating reinterpretation of Century III, Quatrain 60. It suggests that China will mobilize a massive army, and become even more influential in Asia Minor, where Mysia, Lycia and Pamphalia are located. Today, Iran, Iraq and Turkey are part of Asia Minor. There is little doubt that China has become friendly towards some of the anti-Western governments in the region, and even sold high-tech military and nuclear material to the despots of the area. In this scenario, the last lines refer not to the Antichrist, but to his enigmatic predecessor.

Again, in Century IV, Quatrain 47, Nostradamus speaks of an evil 'dark' one, somehow linked to the third Antichrist and the madness he sparks.

Left:. Nostradamus uses comets to date several of his predictions. Most commentators on the quatrains assume that he was always referring to Halley's comet, but its 76-year periodicity was only established nearly 200 years after Nostradamus's death. Most comets appear much less regularly.

"When the ferocious dark one will have exercised
His bloody hand through fire, the sword, the drawn bow,
All the nation will be so terrified to see
The great ones hanging by their neck and feet."

"'The power of Rome will be quite put down,
Following the footsteps of its great neighbour.
Secret hatreds and civil disputes
Will delay the stupidities of the buffoons.'
Century III Quatrain 63

Previously, this was thought to refer to the relationship between Italy and Germany in the time of Mussolini and Hitler. But new research hints it could refer to the terrorist leader, Abu Abbas, whose barbaric acts could help usher in the age of the third Antichrist. As John Hogue argues, "Sometimes Nostradamus hid the name of a perpetrator in a verb. In French, to 'put down' is 'abas'. Certainly Italian international prestige was damaged first when the Achille Lauro was hijacked in October of 1985, and later when Italian authorities allowed Abu 'Ab(b)as' to leave the country and therefore escape arrest."

In this age of terrorism, some of Nostradamus' predictions have become more clear. Originally, most scholars saw little chance of ever deciphering Century X, Quatrain 96, which reads:

'The religion named after the seas will overcome,
Against the sect of the son of Adaluncatif:
The obstinate, deplored sect will be afraid
Of the two wounded Aleph and Aleph (Alif).'

Now, however, an answer to this mystery may have been revealed. Some analysts say it refers to the downing of Pan Am flight 103, though the reasoning is tenuous. They claim the word 'Adaluncatif' contains an anagram for Cadafi Luna ... or Gaddafi of the Moon (the crescent moon is a symbol of Islam). The two men could be the suspects wanted by the west for prosecution in the bombing.

Although there is much room for doubt as to the actual identity of the third Antichrist, there is little reason to doubt that he will strike at the very heart of civilization and cause "a horrible

MASTER OF TERROR

Abu Nidal is without doubt the most cold-blooded and brutal terrorist operating in the world today. In 1972, after splitting with Yassar Arafat's PLO the previous year, he became involved with the notorious Black September group that killed Israeli athletes at the Munich Olympic Games. Throughout the decade, his shadowy group, which came to bear his *nom de guerre*, was responsible for atrocities throughout Europe and the Middle East. It was not until the mid-1980s that he became the master terrorist, surpassing the exploits of the infamous Carlos the Jackal. Although he commands a ragtag – though highly-disciplined – army of followers numbering no more than 1,000 men, he has been involved in a slew of terrorist acts, including the assassinations of many moderate Arab leaders – usually 'traitors' who spoke of peace with Israel or simply slighted him in some real or imaginary way. He has already passed a death sentence on Arafat, whom he considers the Judas of the Palestinian cause.

Apart from attacks on Israelis and sympathetic Arabs, Abu Nidal has also struck deep into the heart of western life. On his orders, people have been shot down as they prayed in temples and bombed as they sipped coffee in Parisian restaurants. He also organized the twin massacres at Rome and Vienna airports in 1985. Security experts estimate that, although his group is relatively few in numbers, it enjoys widespread support from some governments in the area and is hired out as a modern-day Murder Incorporated by various Middle Eastern thugs. It's said that Abu Nidal, whose group is worth some $100 million, also demands extortion money from regimes in the Moslem world. Indeed, it's been revealed that Colonel Moammar Gaddafi pays the group several million dollars a year not to conduct any missions on his soil, while the wealthy Saudi Arabians may have handed over a whopping $15 million to him for his assurances not to sabotage efforts during Operation Desert Storm.

Right: This picture of Sabri Al Banna, more famously known as Abu Nidal, was taken in Beirut in 1982. It is one of the most recent published pictures of a man who is one of the most wanted terrorists in the world. Will the third antichrist be a terrorist rather than a political leader?

slaughter." The most likely scenario, according to the latest research, is that Mabus will somehow get his hands on a nuclear device – either by stealth or under the sanction of a friendly regime – and then use it against defenceless citizens. Nostradamus warns of such a horrible future in several quatrains, in which he appears to see several different incidents that may well be part of a third world war:

"When weapons and plans are enclosed
in a fish
When Mars and Mercury are in conjunction
with Pisces.
Out will come a man who will then
make war.
His fleet travelled far across the sea to appear
on the Italian shore."
Century II Quatrain 5

Nostradamus speaks of an attack on Italy, from man who uses submarine – 'fish' – warfare. A submarine attack, using nuclear weapons, is hardly science fiction today. However, it is also perfectly possible that the first line is a prosaic rendering of the first. In astrological terms, Mars represents agression ('weapons') and Mercury mental activity ('plans'), while the constellation Pisces is symbolized as two fish.

"Through lightning in a box gold and silver
are melded.
The two captives will devour each other.
The greatest one of the city stretched
When the fleet travels under water."

Century III Quatrain 13

This quatrain again suggests an attack on Italy, or more precisely Rome – 'the greatest one' being the Pope.

"After great misery for mankind, an even
greater
Approaches when the great cycle of the
centuries is renewed.
It will rain blood, milk, famine, war and
disease.
In the sky will be seen a fire, dragging a great
trail of sparks."

Century II Quatrain 46

Here Nostradamus speaks of the turn of the century – when the cycle is renewed – which backs up his earlier predictions that some catastrophe engineered by the third Antichrist will come in 1999. The images he conjures up are truly terrifying.

"During the appearance of the bearded star
The three great princes will be made enemies.
The shaky peace on earth shall be struck from
the skies;
The Po, the winding Tiber, a serpent placed
on the shore."

Century II Quatrain 43

According to John Hogue, the bearded star may be a new comet yet unseen by earth's telescopes. The three princes may

stand for the First, Second and Third Worlds, or a pact between three nations that support terrorist activities and will one day war among themselves. An attack from the skies is something of which Nostradamus warns us constantly throughout this period of history.

As Hogue sees it, "The future may see a Libyan or other Arab country's submarine under cover of darkness deposit a band of PLO commandos and their metaphorical 'serpent' – a metaphor for a stolen nuclear device or homemade atom bomb – off the Italian coast at the mouth of the Tiber River. Even a nuclear plant in Northern Italy's Po river region could be the scene of a terrorist attack. One of Italy's two nuclear power plants is at Caorso, a town two miles south of the Po river near Cremona."

"The Antichrist very soon annihilates
the three
Seven and twenty years his war will last.
The unbelievers are dead, captive, exiled:
With blood, human bodies, water and red hail
covering Earth."

Century VIII Quatrain 77

This implies that the third Antichrist will wage – or possibly just trigger – a war lasting 27 years, which would obviously make World War II a 'minor' incident by comparison. However, it is difficult to see how a nuclear war could last so long. The three annihilated could be the Kennedy brothers, who fought against totalitarianism all their lives, or indeed the 'three princes' who featured in the previous quatrain.

The spectre that hangs over mankind is clear, say those who believe in the predictions of Nostradamus. Somewhere in the world today is the last man-beast, whose deeds will bring far more ruin to our planet than ever imagined.

He may be someone like Saddam Hussein, a national leader whose mad quest for power sets off an epic battle between the Christian and Moslem worlds. He could be a skulking arch-terrorist, like Abu Nidal, who with one shocking stroke sets in motion a series of events which lead us irrevocably to war. Or he could be someone who, in the next three years, comes to power by trickery or chance, and turns his demonic gaze to conquest.

CHAPTER SIX

In Our Own Time

'The evil century'

◇

Many of the newest interpretations of Nostradamus's mysterious quatrains involve events this century. That is to be expected - but not necessarily welcome, because most of them suggest a terrible end to this decade. In this chapter, we will learn that the great prophet even suggests where the conflagration will begin with a revised look at the enigmatic mention of the word "Raypoz".

Modern research also changes our ideas about what Nostradamus was trying to tell us about the Kennedy assassination, his belief that there could be yet another war in the Middle East, where we might look for a cure for AIDS and the destruction of the space shuttle Challenger.

But his works have also been reinterpreted to suggest he foresaw great natural calamities coming in the immediate years ahead which will wipe out millions.

Nostradamus saw visions covering hundreds of years, yet he paid particular attention to the 20th century, which he called 'the evil century'. He predicted it would be plagued by three world wars and mass destruction. But the great seer of Salon saw more to our time than just war and chaos. Indeed, he foretold everything from the birth of Israel to the assassination of the Kennedy brothers to the scourge of AIDS to the Challenger disaster. He saw the past 50 years spread before him as in a textbook of modern history.

In this chapter, we will examine – in chronological order – some of his most startling visions of our time; those past, and those yet to come.

"Pestilences extinguished, the world becomes small
For a long time the lands will be inhabited in peace.
People will travel safely by air, over land, seas and wave.
Then wars will start again."

Century I Quatrain 63

Following the end of World War II, many nations settled down to enjoy the fruits of rebirth in the 1950s, when economies boomed in the west. Around the same time, people began to travel en masse, taking to the skies in great passenger airliners, covering great distances in just hours – which indeed made the world feel a lot smaller. But notice Nostradamus's warning in the last line. Following the few years of peace, the ravages of war began to devastate civilization anew.

"Newcomers build a place without defence,
Occupying a place until then uninhabitable.
Meadows, houses, fields, towns to take at pleasure,
Famine, plague, war, extensive arable land."

Century II Quatrain 19

Here is the birth of the state of Israel, which came into being on 14 May 1948. The newcomers are those European Jews who escaped the Nazi gas chambers – as well as Zionists from the USA and those fleeing persecution in the USSR – and flocked to Palestine after World War II.

As Nostradamus notes, the Israelis, whose kibbutzes were ill-defended against Arab attackers, turned their nation from a desert into an oasis. In the last two lines of the quatrain, he may be giving the people of Israel a warning not to become tyrants to those they conquered in the many wars against the Arab states.

"A new law will occupy a new land
Around Syria, Judea and Palestine.
The great barbarian empire will crumble
Before the century of the Sun is finished."

Century III Quatrain 97

In this quatrain, Nostradamus notes precisely the location of Israel, born in the aftermath of World War II. Although the second half of the prophecy remains unfulfilled, it is forecast to happen by the end of this century. Nostradamus calls

---

Below: The birth of the State of Israel with the proclamation of a provisional government in Palestine was marked in Washington DC by the unfurling of the new nation's flag outside the Jewish Agency.

BIRTH OF A NATION

The creation of Israel was marked by years of fighting between armed Jewish groups and British forces, who had the uneasy task of trying to maintain order in Palestine while World War II raged around them. Tensions between Arabs and Jews intensified after the war, as thousands of Jews moved back to their ancestral homelands. As the stampede gathered momentum, Jewish terror groups in Palestine stepped up their attacks against British targets, hoping to force the issue of an independent state of Israel. British subjects were killed; 28 died in a single bomb attack on the King David Hotel in Jerusalem in July 1946.

Sickened by the growing fanaticism in the area, the British government finally washed its hands of the whole thing in 1947, and informed Jewish leaders it was turning the problem over to the United Nations. Once the British had gone, the idea of a Jewish state became increasingly popular in the USA. President Harry S Truman supported the agitation for two reasons; he was genuinely in favour of the idea, and believed he needed the Jewish vote to win the 1948 election. With his backing, a scheme to partition Palestine was passed by the United Nations in November 1947. This soon led to armed conflict with the neighbouring Arabs.

With an army of barely 20,000, Israel was taking on forces far superior in numbers and equipment. David Ben-Gurion, premier of the fledgling state, knew he needed to act decisively – and quickly – if Israel was to survive its infancy. In April 1948, just one month before the new nation of Israel was declared, he launched a pre-emptive strike against the enemies that surrounded him. The plan worked, and the nation survived its first major crisis. In the aftermath of this, more than half a million Jews living in the neighbouring Arab countries were expelled – most of them went to Israel – while an equal number of Arab refugees were displaced from the Jewish state. Instead of trying to assimilate the refugees, the Arab countries kept their disgruntled brethren in camps, thereby helping to fan the flames of hatred towards Israel that led to the outbreak of three more wars in the next 25 years.

the Arab countries that surround Israel 'barbarian' and warns they will be beaten by the year 2001. Amazingly, over the past 20 years we have seen many of the Arab countries end their state of war with Israel and offer their former enemy an olive branch. Egypt, Saudi Arabia, Jordan, and most recently the Palestinians have all turned away from war or 'barbarity', and there are currently moves afoot to end the hostilities between Israel and Syria.

"At that time Cyprus will be deprived of its help
From those of the Aegean Sea.
Old men slaughtered; but by cannons and supplications,
The King is won over; the queen more outraged."

Century III Quatrain 89

During the 1950s, there was terrorist action in British-controlled Cyprus, as the ethnic Greek population sought

Enosis – Union – with Greece, a move resisted both by the British and the island's sizeable Turkish population. Later, Constantine, the Greek king, was forced into exile, and his mother, Queen Frederika, never forgave those who forced the family to flee their kingdom.

Above: David Ben-Gurion's slight stature and avuncular features belied his strength of will and his steely resolve to establish an independent Jewish state.

Left: The heady optimism that had pervaded Budapest after Premier Nagy's declaration of independence in November 1956 evaporated into bitter fighting when the Russians retaliated.

"Through life and death, the rule of Hungary changed.
The law will be more harsh than slavery.
Their great city calls out with howls and laments,
Castor and Pollux are enemies in the arena."

Century II Quatrain 90

The tumultuous events of 1 November 1956 did not go unnoticed by the prophet, who in this quatrain clearly sees the brief though bloody revolt of the Hungarians against their Communist overlords. On that day, Premier Imre Nagy declared that Hungary would no longer tolerate Soviet dominance and withdrew his nation from the Warsaw Pact – the communist alliance that confronted NATO throughout the Cold War. For three days, Hungarians thought they had achieved the impossible in breaking the yoke of Moscow, but the Russian tanks rumbled into the cities to quell the uprising. Fighting broke out on the streets of Budapest, pitting rebellious Hungarians not only against Soviet troops but against their communist compatriots – hence the reference to Castor and Pollux, the twin brothers of Greek and Roman mythology. After the rebellion was put down, the Soviets instituted an even more savage rule over Hungary, trying and executing thousands of rebels, including the heroic Nagy.

"The lands populated by humans
Will become uninhabitable
Nations given to men incapable of prudence.
For the three brothers, death and dissension."

Century II Quatrain 95

This is one of several quatrains dealing with the Kennedy brothers, referred to in the last line. The first three lines depict the turmoil against which the siblings fought all their lives, but most researchers could never reconcile the number of brothers killed in the struggle against chaos with actual history. Although John and Bobby fell victim to assassins' bullets, Senator Edward Kennedy is very much alive and well – although his ultimate political ambitions were destroyed by the Chappaquiddick incident. Who then is this third brother? New thinking is that the third brother of the quatrains is the the oldest Kennedy son, Joseph, who was killed fighting the Nazis – the followers of Nostradamus's second Antichrist – in World War II.

THE FIRST BROTHER

Joseph Kennedy Jr, the eldest child of Joseph and Rose Kennedy, was groomed by the family to become President of the United States from an early age. He was very much his father's favourite, and excelled in both academic and leadership challenges while at school and Harvard. Like his younger brothers, he had a large appetite for women and good times – despite his intense Catholicism – and would often steal John's girlfriends. Nevertheless, he was tremendously popular within the family, and adored by John, despite their rivalry. Even his father's many enemies took a liking to the outgoing Joe Jr.

When the United States entered World War II after the sneak attack on Pearl Harbor, Joe took time out from his fun-loving lifestyle and open pronouncements of one day sitting in the White House to join the Navy as a pilot. John followed him into the navy, and Joe was more than a little miffed when his younger brother came to outrank him. The rivalry was further intensified when John was proclaimed a war hero after his patrol boat was bombed by the Japanese and he dragged survivors to safety. Joe, too, was a brave and fearless fighter. After completing two tours of duty and flying some 50 missions over European waters, he was eligible to return home, but rejected the hard-won right, and volunteered for an experimental mission, flying a Liberator bomber heavily laden with explosives, from which he would bail out once a control plane had directed it to its target. Tragically, something went terribly wrong – the incident is still shrouded in mystery – and the Liberator exploded while still over English soil.

Joe's death had a profound effect on the Kennedy clan, especially John and Joe Sr. As John later wrote, "I think that if the Kennedy children ever amount to anything, it will be due more to Joe's behaviour and his constant example that to any

Above: Joseph and Rose Kennedy had five daughters and four sons, who at one time seemed set to establish a dynasty in American politics. However, three of the boys would die violently; Joe Junior (back row), John (left) and Bobby (front).

other factor." His father was utterly inconsolable. For months following the tragedy, he hardly left his house or spoke to anyone, sitting alone in his study listening to classical music.

Many years later, Joe Sr still could not bring himself to speak about his dead son. In 1957, when a newspaper reporter asked him to describe Joe Jr, the old man broke down and wept. "It was a terrible thing to see," said the newsman. "He sat there at the table weeping, unable to speak or to control himself, for almost five minutes. It seemed to the rest of us like an hour. Finally, he pulled himself together and wiped his eyes, but still he couldn't talk. He gestured towards his wife and said, 'She can tell you about him. I can't.'"

"The great man will be struck down in the day by a thunderbolt,
The evil deed predicted by the bearer of a petition.
According to the prediction another falls at night time.
Conflict in Reims, London and pestilence in Tuscany."

Century I Quatrain 26

Here, Nostradamus foretells the murders of both John and Bobby Kennedy. The president was killed at lunchtime on 22 November 1963 in Dallas. Bobby was shot in the early hours of 6 June 1968 in a Los Angeles hotel kitchen shortly after delivering a victory speech after his win in the California primary election. The 'evil deed' of John's murder was indeed predicted by a more modern seer, Jeane Dixon, who kept trying to warn the president until his death. The last line refers to the turmoil around the time of Bobby's assassination, when student riots erupted in France and London, and a great flood in Florence led to fears of a widespread plague.

Above and below: The surviving Kennedy brothers seemed to have the world at their feet at the end of the 1950s, but in the space of the next dozen years John was assassinated, Edward tainted by scandal and Robert shot dead in a hotel basement in Los Angeles.

Nostradamus again touches on the assasination of John Kennedy in Century II, Quatrain 57.

"Before the battle the great man will fall,
The great one killed, death too sudden and lamented.
Born imperfect, he will go the great part of the way;
Near the river the ground is stained with blood."

Kennedy's death was certainly sudden and lamented by people the world over. The imperfection probably refers to his chronic back condition, or his constant womanizing while in the White House. Erika Cheetham believes the phrase in the remainder of the third line refers to the Cuban missile crisis, when Kennedy went head-to-head with Soviet premier Nikita Krushchev, bringing the world to the brink of nuclear war.

Nostradamus saw the events surrounding President Kennedy's murder in much greater detail in other quatrains, and even the mystery surrounding the actual assassin – or assassins.

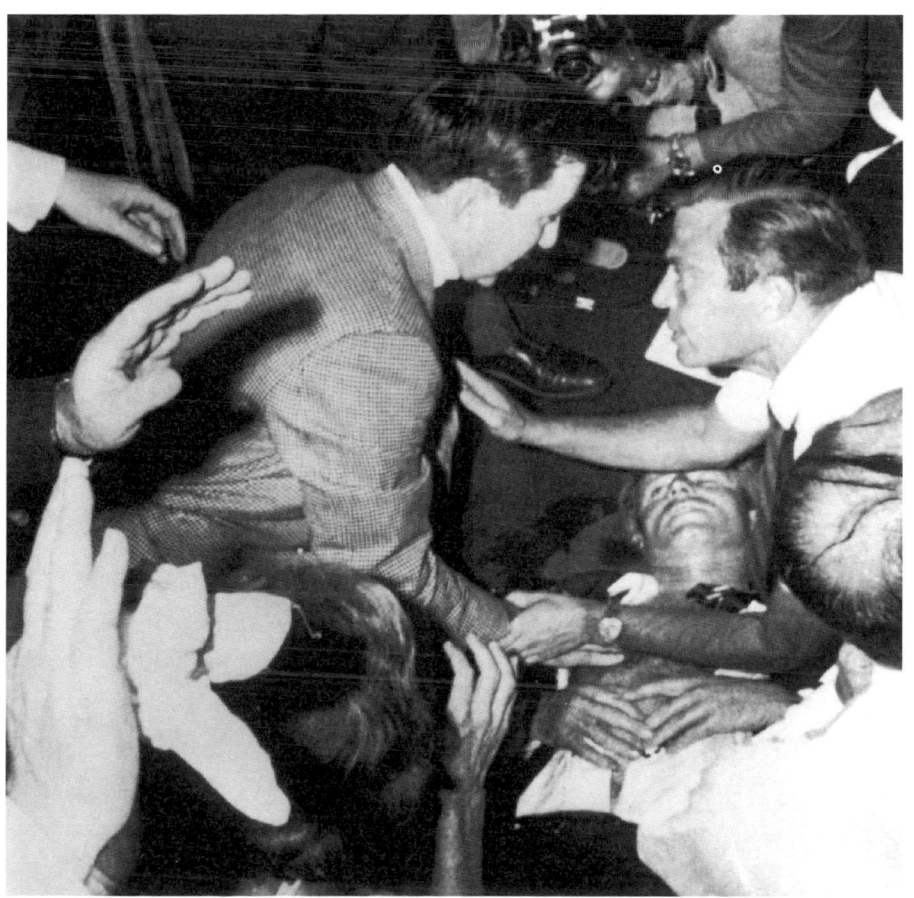

A TRIBUTE TO
ROBERT FRANCIS
KENNEDY
ONE DOLLAR

The Assassination—The Funeral • A Nation Mourns A Fallen Leader
The Hope and Dream of Youth • The Man and His Family
His Search for Knowledge and Understanding • The Statesman—
Servant of the People • His Greatness and Humility — An Appreciation

Left: Bobby Kennedy's murder in 1968 shocked the world. Though Sirhan Sirhan was convicted of acting alone, doubts persist about the role of the Mob and a security man standing behind Kennedy when he was shot.

Below: President Kennedy insisted on riding through Dallas in an open-topped car so he could be seen clearly by his supporters, though he had powerful enemies in the city. The decision cost him his life.

To this day, few Americans have ever believed the findings of the Warren Commission, set up by the incoming President Lyndon Johnson to investigate the assassination of John Kennedy, which concluded that Lee Harvey Oswald acted alone. Indeed, even official reports by the U.S. Congress in recent years have concluded that there was a conspiracy in the assassination of the president. Many people even believe that Oswald was innocent, or at least a minor member of a conspiracy that set him up as a 'patsy' or scapegoat. Of course, had they read Nostradamus, they would have already known that.

> *"The ancient work will be accomplished,*
> *And from the roof evil ruin will fall on the*
> *great man.*
> *Being dead they will accuse an innocent*
> *of the deed;*
> *The guilty one hidden in the misty woods."*
>
> Century VI Quatrain 37

The 'ancient work' referred to in the quatrain is the murder of a king, or in our times, a president. Nostradamus

Right: The shooting of Oswald suggested that Kennedy was the victim of a conspiracy. Jack Ruby had links with the Mafia and no obvious motive for his action.

implies that Oswald, who was gunned down and killed two days later by a Dallas club-owner, Jack Ruby, while he was in police custody, was innocent of the crime, while the guilty one lay in wait for the president 'in the misty woods'. This is a stunning line, because immediately after the murder, many people who were in Dealey Plaza that day said they heard shots coming from a clump of trees behind a grassy knoll, rather than from the high window in a

San Francisco Chronicle
THE VOICE OF THE WEST

99th YEAR No. 329   FINAL HOME EDITION ★   MONDAY, NOVEMBER 25, 1963   10 CENTS   GArfield 1-1111

Oswald Shot Dead
By Dallas 'Avenger'

The Killer Strikes

Single Bullet

Fatal Attack As Police Move Accused Man

Dallas
A.P. & U.P.
Lee Harvey Oswald, accused assassin of President Kennedy, was shot and killed while being transferred from one jail to another yesterday, 48 hours after the death of the President.

He had never wavered in his insistence that he was not the President's killer. He died without saying a word.

The man who shot Oswald, Jack Ruby, 52, bachelor owner of two Dallas night clubs, had stepped swiftly through a mass of police and newsmen at a basement garage ramp in city hall.

He rushed up to Oswald and sent a single pistol bullet into his abdomen.

Oswald dropped unconscious at Ruby's feet, within a cordon of escorting police officers.

At least eight police
See Page 1-C, Col. 5

JACK DAVIS DEEPLY MOURNS AND

S. F. Stands Still Today To Mourn

SECRETS OF THE KENNEDY CONSPIRACY

There have been numerous theories surrounding the conspiracy to kill President John F. Kennedy – pointing the finger at everyone from Nikita Krushchev to the CIA.

There is no doubt that the Soviet leader, Krushchev, had been embarrassed by the young President over the Cuban missile crisis. Those who believe the Soviets were behind the assassination note that Oswald lived in Russia for more than two years, had no trouble returning to the United States with his Soviet-born wife, and was seen visiting the Soviet embassy in Mexico City a few months before the murder. Was Oswald a KGB assassin? The question raged for more than two decades, but under the democratic reforms of Mikhail Gorbachev and Boris Yeltsin, many of the KGB's secret files have been opened – including the one tracking Oswald's movements in the USSR. There is nothing there to suggest Oswald was a Soviet agent, or that any Soviet citizen played a role in the murder – something Moscow asserted from the beginning. In fact, the latest evidence suggests that the KGB considered Oswald a unstable, dim-witted paranoid – hardly the sort of ace assassin the heads of the Soviet secret police would pick for the most sensational murder of the century.

It's no secret that the Mafia had the motive – and the muscle – to kill President Kennedy. Organized crime figures were furious with John and his brother, Attorney General Robert Kennedy, over the their efforts to crack down on the Mob. According to attorney Frank Ragano, who was close to the powerful and corrupt president of the Teamsters' Union, Jimmy Hoffa, the President's murder was organised by New Orleans crime czar Carlos Marcello and Florida mob chief Santos Trafficante. Trafficante headed the once-lucrative Cuban operations for the Mafia, while Marcello had actually been deported to Guatemala by the crusading Bobby. Ragano says he met with Hoffa in early 1963, and "Jimmy told me to tell Marcello and Trafficante they had to kill the president."

Ragano thought Hoffa was joking, but when he mentioned it to the two mobsters a few days later, "They didn't laugh. They were dead serious." The night Kennedy was killed, Ragano said Hoffa, Trafficante and Marcello all celebrated as if there was no tomorrow. Another pointer to Mafia involvement is that Jack Ruby, the man who silenced, Oswald, was known to have underworld connections.

In the late 1970s, a Congressional probe into the murder of JFK concluded – though it could not prove – that Kennedy may have been killed by a deadly alliance of mobsters and anti-Castro Cubans, who felt the president had abandoned them in attempts to get rid of Castro.

Could Fidel Castro have been the mastermind? The Cuban dictator and President Kennedy were avowed enemies and their hatred of each other was palpable. Kennedy, like subsequent American presidents, abhorred the idea of a Soviet client state just 100 miles from the U.S. coastline, and even sanctioned the botched Bay of Pigs invasion in an attempt to start a counter-revolution. Castro, not surprisingly, never forgave Kennedy for allowing the invasion to go ahead, but became even more furious when an unholy alliance of the CIA, the Mafia and exiled Cubans tried to have him killed. The despot held Kennedy responsible for the assassination attempts, and those who support the Castro connection say the Cuban leader decided to kill the president before another attempt could be made.

Still others say responsibility for the assassination lies with the military-industrial complex. This theory claims that Oswald – or others – were actually CIA agents working in cahoots with the U.S. military and greedy weapons manufacturers. Believers hold that Kennedy was trying to scale back U.S. involvement in the burgeoning Vietnam conflict, and that an elite group of arch-conservatives decided to kill him so the war could be escalated. In fact, just days prior to JFK's visit to Dallas, a group of anti-Communist Texas businessman began running newspaper advertisements calling for Kennedy's impeachment for treason. Other far right-wing businessmen were also upset with Kennedy's civil rights program, because he aggressively fought for, and upheld, the rights of America's black population.

warehouse from which Oswald supposedly fired three shots. Strangely, many of those witnesses later died violent and mysterious deaths. Pictures of the area from which they said the shots came were later enhanced to depict what looked like the outline of a rifle barrel protruding through the branches. Will the real killer – or killers – of President Kennedy ever be known? Nostradamus indicates they will.

"Before the people, blood will be spilt,
It will not come far from the high heavens:
But for a long time it will not be heard,
The spirit of a single man will bear witness
to it."

Century IV Quatrain 49

Some people originally thought the man who would reveal the true story behind the assassination might be Ruby, who was sentenced to life in prison for killing Oswald. Ruby, who at first made the preposterous claim that he murdered Oswald to spare Jackie Kennedy the agony of having to return to Dallas and testify at a trial, never did reveal what he knew – only that the truth would never come out. Indeed, he admitted to members of the Warren Commission that "The world will never know the true facts of what occurred because unfortunately, the people who had so

Above: The death of President Kennedy was a personal, as well as a public tragedy, but only the beginning of decades of further suffering – of murder, scandal, alcoholism and marital break-up – for the Kennedy family.

much to gain will never let the true facts come out, above board, to the world."

Who are the people who had so much to gain? There was the Mafia, angered by the Kennedy administration's crackdown on organized crime and his failure to overthrow Fidel Castro in Cuba, where the mob had once raked in tens of millions of dollars annually in gambling casinos. CIA veterans and Cuban exiles were also upset with Kennedy over his refusal to provide military and air support for the botched invasion of Cuba at the Bay of Pigs. Then there was the giant military-industrial complex, which hated Kennedy for his apparent decision to pull out of Vietnam, thereby costing them a fortune in government contracts.

"Six days the assault is made in front of the city.
Freedom is attained in a strong and bitter fight.
Three will hand it over and to them pardon;
To the rest fire, and bloody slashing and slaughter."

Century III Quatrain 22

SECRETS OF THE SIX DAY WAR

The Six Day War of June 1967 began just a few weeks after the United Nations security force abandoned the area at the request of Egyptian President Gamal Abdel Nasser. Two days later, Cairo Radio announced, "This is our chance, Arabs, to deal Israel a mortal blow of annihilation." Troops from Egypt, Syria and Jordan began massing along the borders with Israel, and the inevitability of war again clouded the horizons of the Middle East.

However, following the example of former leader David Ben-Gurion in 1948, the Israelis launched a pre-emptive strike against their enemies on 4 June. First they took out the much-vaunted Egyptian air force before the planes had time to scramble into the air, then they dealt similar blows to air bases in Jordan and Syria. In just six days, the Arab nations were entirely routed and Israel trebled its territory, occupying the Sinai, West Bank and the Golan Heights, whence the Syrians had launched earlier attacks against Jewish settlers.

Most important of all to the victorious Israelis, Jerusalem was now totally in their hands, giving Jews the world over access to their most sacred sites, including the Wailing Wall. After the hostilities ended, a shaky cease-fire was enacted between the warring parties, but in 1969 Nasser broke the pact and began a 'war of attrition' against Israel, using Soviet-made artillery to fire on Israeli forces occupying the east bank of the Suez Canal. A year later, the USA persuaded Nasser to desist and accept the cease-fire agreement. He died three months later.

Above: The lightning speed of the pre-emptive strikes launched by the Israelis, coupled with their superior weaponry, brought the war to a swift conclusion.

The conflict between Israel and its Arab neighbours in 1967 lasted just six days, with a complete victory for the young nation which captured its sacred city, Jerusalem. The three who 'hand it over' and then gain pardon might be Egypt, Jordan and Syria. Only the last of these has yet to sign a peace accord with Israel, and there are indications now that Tel Aviv and Damascus are moving towards a peace agreement. The last line is probably a reference to those Moslem nations in the Middle East and Africa that refuse to accept Israel's right to existence, such as Libya, Iraq and Iran. For them, Nostradamus sees nothing but turmoil, perhaps in another war to come.

Above and right: Nostradamus's prediction of the American moon landings, pioneered in 1969 by Neil Armstrong, Michael Collins and 'Buzz' Aldrin in Apollo 11, is among the most dazzling of his prophecies.

"He will come to take himself
To the corner of Luna
Where he will be taken and placed
On an alien land."

Century IX Quatrain 65

This is probably the most remarkable quatrain Nostradamus ever wrote about our time. There can be no doubt that he saw man walking on the Moon – Luna is the Latin name for it. More than 400 years before the world sat and watched in awe as American astronaut Neil

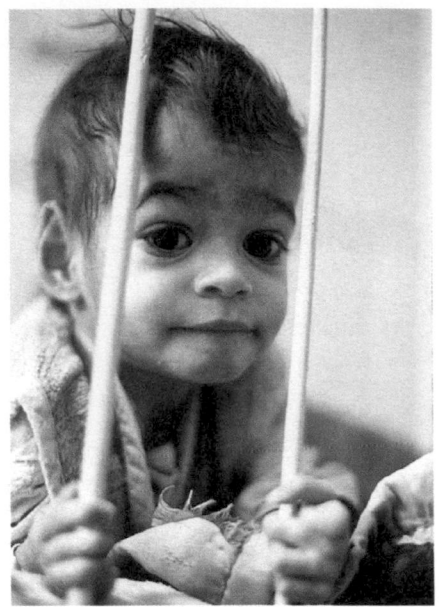

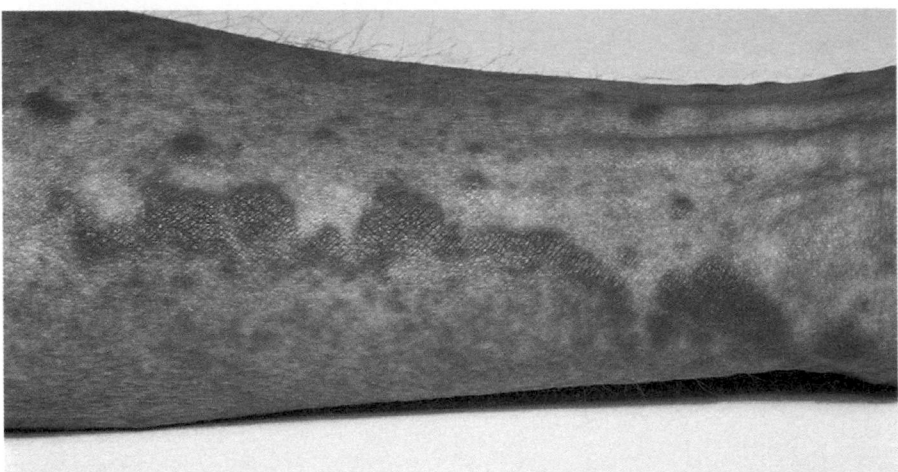

Since the disease was named in the early 1980s, AIDS has become a worldwide scourge, though not so much as diseases such as tuberculosis. Children whose mothers are infected often have the virus, and skin lesions – or scars, as Nostradamus called them – due to once-rare diseases have become commonplace.

Armstrong made his historic landing in July 1969, Nostradamus saw it all unfold before him in his study. And if we were stunned by the achievement – which just 20 years earlier was the stuff of science fiction – just imagine how a 16th-century doctor felt!

In the years surrounding this magnificent achievement, a previously unknown virus was gaining a foothold in an unsuspecting world. Today, we know the virus as the cause of AIDS – Acquired Immune Deficiency Syndrome – which spread from Africa to North America and Europe in the 1960s and early 1970s. For years, no one knew there was such a thing as AIDS, which kills by making the body vulnerable to other diseases. Until 1981, those who died from it were thought to have perished from cancer, pneumonia or one of the other insidious killers it encourages. Since then, there have been hundreds of thousands of deaths attributed to the mystery virus, and the United Nations estimates that at least 15 million people are infected throughout the world, with the numbers growing every day.

A Modern Plague

Did Nostradamus see this modern-day scourge? There is evidence to support those who say he did. In Century III, Quatrain 75 he wrote: "Swords damp with blood from distant lands. A very great plague will come with a great scab. Relief near but the remedies far away." Karposi's sarcoma, a previously rare form of skin cancer that is associated with AIDS, creates ugly purple lesions – 'scabs' – on those afflicted. Some modern experts also claim that the 'swords damp with blood' are not a martial reference at all, but are penes; as we now know, the disease is carried in the blood and sexually transmitted. Relief, in the form of drugs and other treatments to ease people through the illness and perhaps slow its course, is at hand, but a cure is still a long way off, say researchers.

Could Nostradamus have been using a double meaning in saying that a remedy was 'far away'?

"A great famine through a pestilent wave,
Will extend over the length of the arctic pole.
Samarobrin, one hundred leagues from
the hemisphere,
They shall live without law, exempt
from politics."

Century VI, Quatrain 5

To understand this quatrain, we must first ascertain what 'Samarobrin' is, 100 leagues – or 300 miles – above the Earth. The only thing that hovers that close to our planet is the Russian space station MIR, which means Peace. In Russian, samo means self, while robin means operator. A space station is indeed self-operated – and is literally far above the

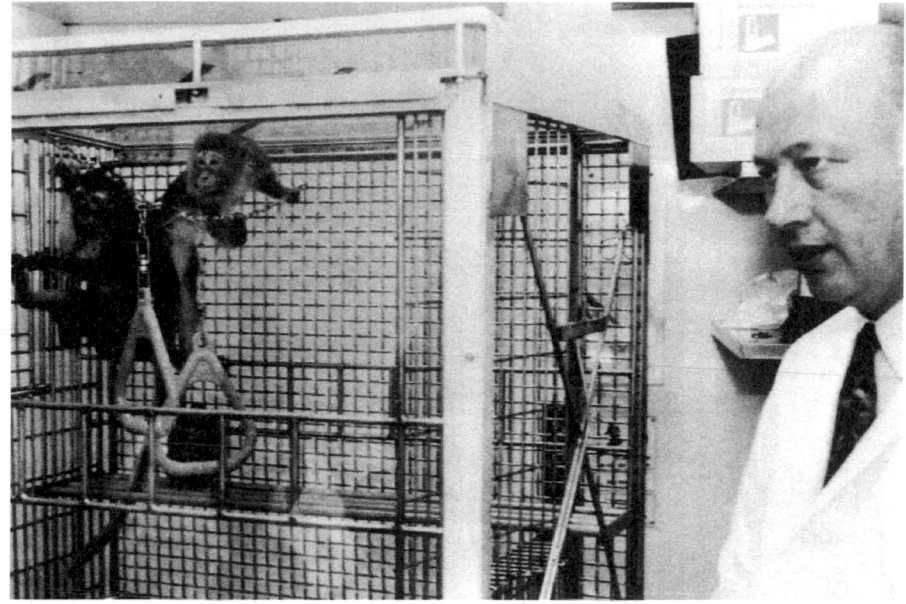

*"Great Neptune from the depths of the sea;
Of mixed African race and French blood,
The islands remain bloody because of the slow one.
It will harm him more than the badly concealed secret."*

The 'slow one' could be a reference to the agonizingly drawn-out, but inexorable progress of the AIDS virus. It's believed the plague began in Africa, and Nostradamus appears to warn it will spread through France and the islands – which could be a reference to Britain.

*"Rain, famine and war will not cease in Persia;
Too great a trust will betray the monarch.
The actions started in France will end there,
A secret sign for one to be sparing."*

Century 1 Quatrain 70

This is a stunning vision of the rise of the fundamentalist cleric, Ayatollah Khomeini, and the fall of the Shah of Iran in 1979. The first line refers to the unrest in Iran (known as Persia in the time of Nostradamus) which preceded the revolution and led directly to end of the Pahlavi dynasty, which the prophet predicts in the second line. If the quatrain foretold only this, it would

confines of man's laws and politics. Could this mean that a cure for AIDS will be found in the heavens through a space-based experiment? We don't yet know what effect zero gravity would have on new vaccines or drugs. Maybe through the mists of time Nostradamus – a healer by profession – may be telling us to look to space for a cure.

Just how huge a toll could AIDS take on mankind? In a frightening letter to Henri II, Nostradamus writes of a plague so vast "that two thirds of the world will fail and decay. So many [will die] that no one will know the true owners of fields and houses. The weeds in the city streets will rise higher than the knees, and there shall be total desolation of the Clergy."

He also gave a warning in Century V, Quatrain 49.

*"Not from Spain but from ancient France,
Will be elected for the trembling ship.
He will make a promise to the enemy
Who will cause great plague during his reign."*

Pope John Paul II hailed from the southwest of Poland, which once marked a boundary of Charlemagne's Holy Roman Empire – 'ancient France'. It has been during John Paul II's reign that the

spread of AIDS first caught the world's attention. Experts are baffled, however, by the joining of the last two lines. Who is the enemy who caused the great plague? Until we discover the exact origins of AIDS, we can never know.

This quatrain has recently been reinterpreted to indicate that Nostradamus might have been speaking of an event yet to come to pass. The suggestion is that there will be two key rivals for the throne of St Peter – from Spain and France – and that the French cardinal will be elected.

Nostradamus also seems to warn of the current AIDS crisis in Century II, Quatrain 78.

THE REBELLIOUS CLERIC

The Ayatollah Khomeini declared the Republic of Islam in February 1979, sending the country hurtling back through the centuries to the time of the prophet Mohammad. During the first two years of his take-over, more than 8,000 people – including children as young as nine years old – were tried, convicted and executed by courts run by fundamentalist zealots for being 'enemies of Allah'. The purge also took in high-ranking members of the Iranian army, including 23 generals and more than 300 other officers. Moreover, religious and ethnic minorities were also targeted for elimination, including Kurds, Christians, Jews, Turkomans and the rival Islamic sect of the Shi'ites, who were predominant in neighbouring Iraq.

However, the Ayatollah did not limit his religious war to those perceived enemies within Iran. He gleefully supported numerous terrorist groups against Israel, Europe and the United States – which he called The Great Satan' – bringing dread to the entire western world. It was his legions who organized the suicide bomb

Above: The British writer, Salman Rushdie, has been in hiding since the Ayatollah Khomeini sentenced him to death for blasphemy in 1989.
Left: Before his triumphant return to Iran, the Ayatollah Khomeini spent many years in a villa in a suburb of Paris, where he led the daily prayers.

The fanaticism of Khomeini also led to the 1989 fatwah or religious ruling against author Salman Rushdie, whose novel *The Satanic Verses* caused a firestorm of controversy throughout the Islamic world. The ruling against Rushdie was sparked in January 1989, when British Moslems held public rallies to burn what they considered to be a blasphemous text. Within a month, news of the book and the outrage was brought to the Ayatollah's attention. He immediately issued a proclamation decreeing that Rushdie had to die. "I

attacks against an American Marine barracks in Beirut on October 1983, killing 241 Marines and almost 60 French troops. He was also believed to be behind another savage attack on U.S. soldiers at a West Berlin night club, and might have shared responsibility for the tragedy of Lockerbie, when an American Pan Am jumbo jet was blown out of the sky over Scotland, killing 269 people.

inform the proud Moslem people of the world that the author of *The Satanic Verses* book, which is against Islam, the Prophet and the Koran, and all those involved in its publication who were aware of its content, are sentenced to death." Although Khomeini himself died in June 1989 at the age of 86, the fatwah on Rushdie is still in place, and Iran remains a pariah nation.

still be a remarkable achievement. Shahs had ruled the Peacock Throne of Persia for thousands of years before Nostradamus was born, and remained firmly in place until 1979. Why would he predict the demise of so entrenched a dynasty – which in his day was as secure as ever – if he did not actually see it? Indeed, even the most sophisticated intelligence agencies, including America's CIA and the KGB of the Soviet Union did not predict the fall of the Shah. How ironic that a man who lived 400 years before the events unfolded saw it all clearly! The last two lines of the quatrain refer to Khomeini, who spent years of exile in France plotting his return and revenge against the monarchy and the establishment of a fundamentalist Moslem state, which he fully achieved.

Below: Ronald Reagan survived the predicted attempt on his life and served a second term as American President.

"The great king captured by the hands of a young man
Not far from Easter. Confusion, incision of the knife.
Everlasting captives, times when the lightning is on the top,
When three brothers will be wounded and murdered."

Century IX Quatrain 36

This quatrain was once thought to have something to do with the Kennedy brothers – Joseph, John and Bobby. The last line certainly appears to, but only in recent years have we grasped the full meaning of the riddle. Today, experts believe it points to the assassination attempt on President Ronald Reagan, which occurred just before Easter in March 1981. The 'young man' is thought to be William Hinckley, the disturbed drifter who thought that if he shot Reagan the actress Jodie Foster

Above: Princess Grace of Monaco was killed in a car crash in 1982. Was the glamorous former film star the person Nostradamus called the 'great golden one'?

would pay attention to him. The 'incision of the knife' is thought to represent the surgery performed on the wounded president. The last line, about the Kennedys, and the third line could mean the general time frame for the attempted killing. The 'everlasting captives' could be the Americans held by Iranian fanatics in Teheran for more than 400 days, or the westerners held captive in Beirut.

"Even greater calamity with blood and famine.
Seven times it approaches the seashore.
Monaco captured, in captivity from hunger.
The great golden one caught in an iron cage."

Century III Quatrain 10

The first three lines of this quatrain appear to be too general to be able to interpret. However, some more modern researchers believe that the last line could be a reference to Princess Grace, who died in a car crash in 1982.

"Nine will be set apart from the human flock
Separated from judgment and counsel;
Their fate will be determined on departure.
Kappa, Theta, Lambda dead, banished
and scattered."

Century I Quatrain 81

This quatrain is thought to refer to the Challenger space shuttle disaster of January 1986. Although seven, rather than nine, American astronauts died when the craft exploded shortly after take-off, it is the last line which has attracted the most attention in recent years. Until recently, no one was sure what the Greek letters 'Kappa, Theta, Lambda' meant, but John Hogue claims to have found the answer. "I would venture that they are an anagram for some of those involved in the Challenger scandal: K, TH, L = (TH)io(K)o(L) = Thiokol." To those unfamiliar with the scandal which erupted in the wake of the disaster, Morton Thiokol was the name of the company that designed and built the rocket booster that failed, causing

the tragedy. As Nostradamus put it in another quatrain, "The unripe fruit will be the source of great scandal." In the investigation that followed, it was revealed that both officials at NASA and at the company did not check the work being done on the boosters more closely. As a result, the craft (or 'unripe fruit') was not properly ready for its mission.

"Thin, tall and dry like reeds, playing the
good valet in the end
Will have nothing but his dismissal.
Sharp poison and letters in his collar,
He will be caught escaping into danger."

Century VIII Quatrain 52

This quatrain baffled experts until recent times. Now it is generally accepted to be a reference to Anthony Blunt, who was revealed as a member of an infamous spy ring that betrayed British secrets to the Soviets. Blunt was the keeper of the royal art collection for Queen Elizabeth II, who was stunned to learn one of her trusted servants was a traitor.

Above: The spectacular explosion of the Challenger space shuttle in 1986 killed seven people and led the USA to rethink its space programme.

Below: The art expert and spy Anthony Blunt was unmasked by Nostradamus 400 years before MI6.

*"Not long after the eclipse of two great moon signs
Which will occur between March and April, what a great loss.
But two great good influences will help on all sides
By land and by sea."*

Century III Quatrain 5

The war between Iran and Iraq – Islamic countries were often referred to in lunar terms by Nostradamus because of the crescent flag – began in 1980. The fighting continued until 1988, causing tens of thousands of casualties. The 'two great good influences' of peace may be a reference to the United Nations and the USA, which both strived long and hard to end the fighting.

*"In those times and areas where the flesh gives way to fish,
The common law will be made in opposition.
The old order will hold strong then be removed from the scene entirely,
All things common among friends put far behind."*

Century IV Quatrain 32

This quatrain tells of the collapse of communism which, until a few years ago, was thought of as impossible, given the power of the Soviet Union and the stranglehold the Kremlin held over what President Ronald Reagan called 'The Evil Empire'. But collapse it did – and in a remarkably short time. The reference to flesh and fish is interesting, because dried fish, as opposed to fresh meat, was the staple food item for the discontented masses in the last, bankrupt days of the USSR. Nostradamus refers to communism as 'All things common among friends'. This is an apt description of the discredited system, which stressed collective ownership of property, farms and industrial plants.

*"Near the Rhine from the Noricum mountains
Will be born a great man of the people, born too late.
He will defend Poland and Hungary
And they will never know what became of him."*

Century III Quatrain 58

Some believe, with little justification, that this quatrain deals with Adolf Hitler and the 'mystery' that they believe surrounds his suicide. Erika Cheetham, however, feels that it concerns a hero rather than an Antichrist. Noricum was the Latin name for Austria, but Lech Walesa was born on the other side of the mountains which separate the country from Poland. The one-time shipyard worker who helped to form the Solidarity movement was indeed a great man of his people, and while he certainly defended his country against the ravages of the communist system, what of the reference to Hungary? Cheetham believes it is there because the freedom movement that Walesa began moved into Hungary, which also threw off the shackles of the totalitarian state and embraced democracy. Could the last line refer to Walesa's recent loss in the Polish elections, meaning he will never again be at the forefront of the democracy he so carefully nurtured through strife, attack and imprisonment?

*"Two revolutions will be caused by the evil scythe bearer,
Making a change in reign and centuries.
The mobile sign of Libra thus moves into its house
Equal in favor to both sides."*

Century I Quatrain 54

One interpretation of this quatrain holds that Nostradamus is speaking of the two revolutions that took place in Russia in 1917, which brought communism – whose emblem was the hammer and sickle (or scythe) – to Russia. The second of these was in October, the month of Libra.

Others believe the reference is to Libra's scales of balance and justice – or democracy, and that the quatrain refers to the end of communism in both Russia and China. Of course it is also perfectly possible that the 'scythe bearer' is the familiar personification of Death as the Grim Reaper, while the 'revolutions' may not be political at all, but a reference to bodies revolving in the heavens. The word was first used to describe violent political change at the end of the 18th century more than 200 years after Nostradamus died.

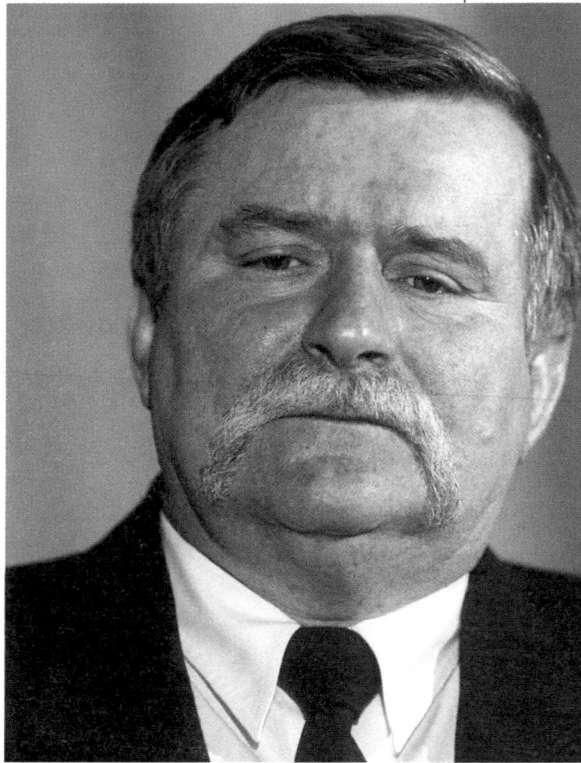

Above: Shipyard worker Lech Walesa was a leader of the pioneering Polish trade union, Solidarity, and became President of Poland after the country was freed from Soviet tyranny.

*"One day, the two great leaders will be friends.
Their great power will be seen to increase.
The new land will be
At the height of its power."*

Century II Quatrain 89

Here, Nostradamus foretells the friendship between the United States and Russia as the chill of the Cold War gives way to new understanding between their leaders and peoples. Today, with the fall of communist dictatorship in the Soviet Union, America – 'the new land' – stands as the last superpower, the strongest nation on Earth. But the friendship will not last too long. Another quatrain suggests it is destined to crumble into a destructive war.

*"The two will not remain allied for long;
Within 13 years they give into Barbary power.
There will be such a loss on both sides, that one will bless
The bark of Peter and the cape of the Pope."*

Century V Quatrain 78

FALL OF THE EVIL EMPIRE

Mikhail Sergeyevich Gorbachev came to power in the Soviet Union at the age of 52 after the death of hardliner Konstantin Chernenko on March 10 1985. A born reformer, he immediately began reorganizing the Communist Party – even though he dismissed the notion of opposition parties as complete nonsense – and set about thawing relations with the west. As he started his massive restructuring of the Soviet economy – which he called *perestroika* – there was rampant inflation, unemployment and a shortage of goods in the stores. The black market continued to flourish, further undermining his plans for restructuring, which was becoming less and less popular with the masses. Gorbachev would not relent, and pressed ahead with his grand vision of new Union, even allowing the media to criticise the Party through *glasnost* or openness.

Under his rule, historians were at last allowed to write about the excesses of Stalin, Jewish dissidents were given more freedom, the KGB was reined in, and fewer citizens were sent to jail for political crimes. But the USSR had sustained itself for 70 years by engendering fear in its subjects. Once Gorbachev eased that dread, there was an increased dissension among the peoples of Russia and the satellite states who were no longer terrified of being dragged off to an internment camp in Siberia. Suddenly, there was a huge increase in crime, worker absenteeism, strikes and alcoholism.

Throughout the late 1980s, there were also rumblings of dissent coming from the republics that made up the Soviet Union. In 1989, the three Baltic states, Estonia, Latvia and

Mikhail Gorbachev (below) was feted by right-wing Western politicians, but his reforms were not so popular at home, eventually bringing about his downfall. Boris Yeltsin (right) replaced him as leader of Russia in 1991.

Lithuania, began to call openly for independence. That fervour soon spread to Georgia and the wealthy Ukraine, already bristling with anti-Soviet sentiment over the Chernobyl meltdown. Despite his popularity with the West, Gorbachev found himself presiding over the break-up of the Union and his popularity at home plummeted. He was eventually challenged for power by Boris Yelstin, who in June 1991 became the first Russian president ever elected by the people.

An early problem for President Gorbachev was the terrible fire at the nuclear reactor in Chernobyl (far left) in 1986, which has left a legacy of sick children (below) throughout the area.

Nostradamus put a lot of importance on Halley's Comet and how it will effect events towards the end of this century. Its last passing was in 1986. If one adds the 13 years (of America and Russia's friendship) to that, we get 1999 – the year Nostradamus predicted the start of World War III. The word 'Barbary' may be a reference to Libya, or indeed the entire Arab world.

The prophet also forecasts giant earthquakes in our very near future, ones that will make the devastating quake that hit San Francisco in 1906 seem gentle by comparison.

"Mars, Mercury and the Moon in conjunction.
Towards the south there will be a great drought.
An earthquake from the bottom of Asia
Corinth and Ephesus in an unstable and troubled state."

Century III Quatrain 3

This giant earthquake will begin its massive rumblings in India, spreading out all the way to Greece (Corinth) and the Arab countries of the Mediterranean (Ephesus). Worse, it could also mean the killer quake could even hit England, which Nostradamus has in other quatrains referred to as Corinth.

Wherever it occurs, this massive upheaval is forecast for when Mars, Mercury and the Moon are in conjunction. The next such astrological alignment will be in March 1998; and after that in July and August 2000. The year 2000 would seem a better bet, given that there will also be a rare planetary alignment – of the moon, the sun, Jupiter and Saturn – on May 5. Scientists are already predicting an increase in unusual natural phenomena around that time due to the subtle gravitational influences being exerted on our planet.

Some now believe that this quatrain – or at least the fourth line – refers instead to tensions between England (Corinth) and Holland (Ephesus). It's even been suggested that the tensions might arise as a result of Holland giving haven to members of the IRA and other terrorist groups. This scenario seems highly unlikely at this point in history, but in the future, who knows?

THE DESTRUCTION OF SAN FRANCISCO

The earthquake that rocked San Francisco in 1906 was one of the worst natural disasters to hit America. Over the course of four fateful days, the City by the Bay was subjected to a series of shocks and fires that claimed the lives of hundreds of people and destroyed many millions of dollars worth of property. San Franciscans have long been forced to acknowledge that their city is a time bomb waiting to explode. It sits on the huge San Andreas Fault, which runs 600 miles along the coastal region of California, extending down to depths of at least 20 miles.

Still, no one was prepared for what happened at precisely 5.12am on 18 April 1906. Seismographs at the University of California in nearby Berkeley were the first to record the shock. The disturbance lasted for 48 seconds, and was felt throughout San Francisco a few minutes later, stopping clocks of buildings in and around the city. Throughout the day, over 120 more shocks rumbled through the area, knocking down stone and wooden buildings as if they were made of cards, and reducing them to piles of rubble and dust. Huge fires swept through the panicked streets as ruptured gas mains ignited.

The fires raged uncontrollably for three days, eventually destroying 514 city blocks in the city's heart and more than 30,000 buildings, prompting one contemporary historian to call it 'the greatest conflagration in historic times'. By the end of the first day, the city was an inferno, and terrified citizens rushed to the surrounding hilltops, where they looked on, helpless, as their homes and offices were consumed by the flames. The fires continued to spread for another 48 hours, so much so that when order was finally restored, the city was little more than an empty shell of debris and ash and 228,000 people were homeless.

The novelist Jack London, a witness to the quake and its aftermath, recalled the scene in a haunting passage. "San Francisco is gone! Nothing remains of it but memories and a fringe of dwelling houses on the outskirts. Its industrial section is wiped out. Its social and residential section is wiped out. The factories and warehouses, the great stores and newspaper buildings, the hotels and the palaces of the nabobs, are all gone.

"Within an hour after the earthquake shock, the smoke of San Francisco's burning was a lurid tower visible a hundred miles away. And for three days and nights, this lurid tower swayed in the sky, reddening the sun, darkening the sky, and filling the land with smoke. There was no opposing the flames. There was no organization, no communication. All the cunning adjustments of a twentieth-century city had been smashed by the earthquake. The streets were humped into ridges and depressions and piled with debris of fallen walls. The steel rails were twisted into perpendicular and horizontal angles. The telephone and telegraph systems were disrupted. And the great water mains had burst. All the shrewd contrivances and safeguards of man had been thrown out of gear by thirty seconds' twitching of the earth's crust."

Above: The 1906 earthquake reduced the mainly wood-built City on the Bay to so much kindling. There were plenty of sparks to catch a fire, and ruptured gas mains fed the flames. The column of fire was visible from as far as 100 miles away.

"A trembling of the Earth at Mortara,
The tin islands of St. George half sunk:
Drowsy with peace, war will awaken,
The abyss of the temple ripped open
at Easter."

Century IX Quatrain 31

This quatrain gives further evidence that the Corinth of the earlier quatrain was indeed Britain – the 'tin islands of St George' – and suggests the Kingdom could be flooded by the great tidal waves which often accompany a major earthquake. The war that has awakened the peoples of the world is World War III, due to begin just months before this cataclysmic quake, which may well be the result of a man-made explosion setting off a chain reaction in the earth's crust.

At the turn of the millennium, Nostradamus sees little but war, famine, plagues and drought.

"The great famine that I sense approaching
Will often appear in different areas, then
become worldwide.
It will be on such an enormous scale and last
such a long time
That roots will be grabbed from trees and
children from the breast."

Century I Quatrain 67

Nostradamus returns to this theme again, in Century II, Quatrain 75:

"The call of the unwelcome bird is heard
On the chimney stack.
Bushels of wheat will rise so high.
As a result, man will devour his fellow man."

During the past 20 years, there have been a series of devastating famines throughout Africa and parts of Asia. But if Nostradamus is right, these terrible plights are just a forerunner of the horrendous one to come.

This famine is so great that it will throw the entire world close to the edge of madness and barbarity, when children are literally torn from the breasts of their mothers for food and cannibalism is rife. In view of the horrors of this quatrain, this would be a good time to remember Nostradamus' warning to us that we can change our future. Maybe if the governments of the world paid more attention to the deterioration of our environment through deforestation and the alarming hole in the ozone layer, we could avoid the worst of the prophet's visions.

Early in the next century – and easily within the lifespan of even most of our senior citizens – another titanic catastrophe will strike the planet, but it will not spring from the bowels of the earth; rather it will come from outer space.

"The great mountain, one mile in
circumference,
After peace, war, famine, flooding.
It will spread far, drowning great countries.
Even antiquities and their mighty
foundations."

Century I Quatrain 69

The 'great mountain' suggests a huge meteorite – perhaps an asteroid or comet – will burst through the Earth's atmosphere and crash into the Mediterranean Sea, near many of the countries of antiquity. The resultant impact will send tidal waves pouring over the land, drowning entire cities and their populations. In another quatrain, Nostradamus warns that the waters will initially rise as high as 1,000 feet above sea level, and that the red-hot steam thrown out of the ocean will half-cook fish around the Italian island of Evvoia.

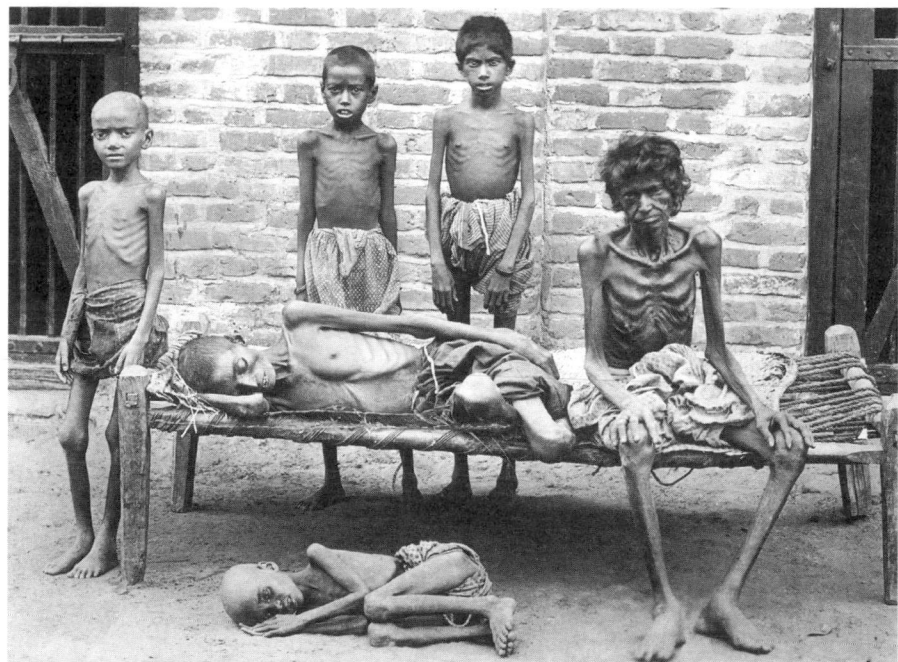

Top: Famine is a common enough obscenity of the 20th century, but Nostradamus predicts that it will spread throughout the world as the new century dawns.

Above: If a large meteorite or comet were to strike the Earth, the debris thrown into the atmosphere would create life-threatening changes to the weather systems.

CHAPTER SEVEN

Into the Next Millennium

What awaits us?

◇

This chapter highlights the dichotomy of horror and hope that Nostradamus foresees for man's future. It has long been believed that he saw only death and destruction for our planet, but the latest research indicates that he also saw a way out for mankind, whatever the horrors to come. That is typical of Nostradamus, who firmly believed we have a choice and that the eventual fate of our planet is in our hands. He said that mankind had the power to alter the future...and if his warnings are any guide, we had better start making the changes needed to secure our survival.

The great seer also speaks of a journey our successors will undertake. Many believe he is referring to a journey of renewal, a new spirituality that will awaken man's soul. However, there is a fresh, bolder interpretation of the same quatrain, suggesting that man's future lies not on this planet, but somewhere out among the stars where all life began. Indeed, Nostradamus pinpoints the precise year this planet could cease to exist, whilst new research into his works implies a belief that mankind will live long after that time.

Since Nostradamus was deeply religious, it makes sense to see his predictions concerning 'a journey' undertaken by mankind sometime in the future as a spiritual trek of renewal. There are dozens of quatrains in which he clearly speaks of spiritual matters that seem relevant to the years after 2000. In an epistle to Henri II, he wrote, "At the eve of another desolation, when the perverted church is atop her most high and sublime dignity ... there will proceed one born from a branch long barren, who will deliver the people of the world from a meek and voluntary slavery ... the flame of the sect shall spread the world over."

There's little doubt that Nostradamus here predicts that organized religions – 'the perverted church' – will eventually give rise to a new faith, born of a long-forgotten branch of Christianity. Although Nostradamus does not say it will be a Christian faith, it would seem implausible, given his religious background, that it would be any other. This new faith will envelop the world, and usher in a reign of peaceful accord.

It is worth noting that Nostradamus also predicted great upheavals within the Catholic Church at the coming of the approaching millennium, which could give rise to this new awakening.

"The new Barque will go on voyages,
Far and near they will transfer the Empire.
Beaucaire and Arles will retain the hostages
Near where the two columns of porphyry
are found."

Century X, Quatrain 93

Above: Arranged mass weddings between followers are a feature of Rev Moon's Unification church.

The money-spinning mix of religion and psychoanalysis cooked up by sci-fi writer L Ron Hubbard (right) has attracted film stars such as John Travolta (opposite left) and Tom Cruise (opposite right).

Left: The Irish saint and seer, Malachy O'Morghair, believed John Paul II would be the last Pope but two.

The Barque is the papacy. Nostradamus is suggesting that a future Pope will one day have to leave the Vatican and move the headquarters of

SECRETS OF THE CELEBRITY SECT

Today, there is an explosion of new religious sects, from those who follow Sun Myung Moon, who founded the Unification Church, to those who believe in the teachings of the New Age gurus. One of the most controversial is the Church of Scientology, founded in the United States 40 years ago by L. Ron Hubbard a popular, though not particularly talented science fiction writer. He claims that through the church's bizarre counselling and psychotherapy sessions – which can cost more than $1,000 an hour – the faithful can overcome everything from blindness to dyslexia, and even improve their appearance and brain power. Hubbard, once branded 'a pathological liar' by a Californian judge, declared that mental problems are caused by 'engrams', the records of past traumas, some from previous existences, and that only by freeing these repressive attitudes could a member find true happiness and enlightenment.

Hollywood stars such as Tom Cruise, Nicole Kidman, John Travolta, Kirstie Alley and Priscilla Presley swear by Scientology's effectiveness.The church has always tried to attract name stars. When Hubbard began the movement, he instantly recognized the value of bringing celebrities to the fold, and started 'Project Celebrity'. Among those he sought to convert to Scientology were Walt Disney, Greta Garbo, Marlene Dietrich, Ernest Hemingway and Howard Hughes. Although these efforts provided unsuccessful, the idea remained, and today the church has a branch, Celebrity Centre International, that caters solely to well-known members. It also has a special office set up to help guide their careers.

Tom Cruise, among the world's biggest box office attractions, has been a member for several years, and says it helped him overcome dyslexia. "It gives me certain tools to utilize to be the person I want to be and explore the areas I want to explore as an artist," he said. "I was always focused on my career, even before I become involved in Scientology. But essentially, it's helped me to become me."

Despite the ridicule it receives from many quarters, Scientology has managed to weather numerous attacks during the course of its history, and no one expects it to suddenly disappear, especially when it has some of the most glamorous and influential devotees in the world and has amassed enormous wealth – which, suggest the sceptics, was the whole point of Hubbard's schemes.

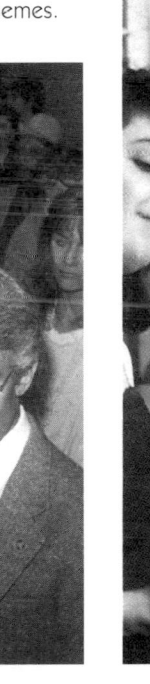

the Catholic Church. Both Beaucaire and Arles are close to the Rhône, near which Pope Pius VI was once held in captivity.

For many hundreds of years before Nostradamus, other seers claimed the Catholic Church would leave Rome near the end of the millennium, possibly as a result of the war just a few years away.

The great Irish prophet, St. Malachy, who lived in the 12th century, is said to have predicted that, after the current pontiff, John Paul II, there would be only two more popes. Around 1140, he travelled to Rome, where he is said to have gone into a trance and proclaimed the popes who would follow the then pontiff Celestinus II. He wrote that, "In the final persecution of the Holy Roman Church, Peter the Roman will occupy the See, who will feed his flock through many tribulations. These tribulations past, the city of seven hills will be destroyed, and the terrible Judge shall judge the people."

Like St Malachy, Nostradamus often refers to the destruction of 'the city of seven hills' – Rome – during the war to come. But if our immediate future looks bleak, there is also hope – hope for a planet and people tired of war and destruction. Indeed, although he sees horrors beyond even our imagination with the coming of the third Antichrist, a third world war and plagues and famines which threaten our very existence, he does appear to contradict some earlier quatrains predicting the end of the world within the next 30 years or so. Maybe it's because he believed that man would awaken to the dangers he has wrought and, heeding the prophet's grave warnings of impending doom, succeed in avoiding Armageddon. It's incredibly difficult to tell for sure, but Century X, Quatrain 84, definitely offers hope.

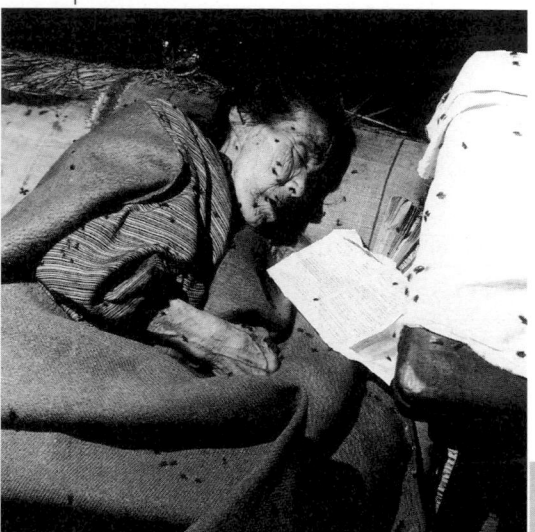

"The walls will change from brick to marble,
Seventy-five peaceful years.
Joy to humankind, the aqueduct reopened.
Health, abundant fruit, joy and mellifluous
times."

Although there is nothing in this quatrain to date the prediction, many believe it foretells of 75 years of peace and plenty following the catastrophe of World War III. Moreover, Nostradamus wrote in a letter to Henri II that "The Antichrist returns for the last time .. All the Christian and infidel nations will tremble ... Wars and battles will be more grievous than ever. Towns, cities, citadels and all other structures will be destroyed. So many evils by Satan's prince will be committed that almost the entire world will find itself undone and desolated. Before these events many rare birds will cry in the air 'Now! Now!', and sometime later will vanish."

Researchers believe that the 'birds' may be a coded key to our survival. They could stand for a man of peace, who will help avert the horrible events that hover over us. Maybe this mysterious person will make mankind

Left and below: Some interpreters believe that Nostradamus's predictions indicate that the suffering and destruction caused by the atomic bomb that fell on Hiroshima is just a faint echo of the third world war to come.

focus on 'Now!' – meaning it is up to our generation to avert the horrors that await us just a few short years away. It's interesting that mystics of the Eastern religions refer to enlightenment as 'now'.

A Golden Age

The latest thinking is that the 'rare birds' represent not a man, but a new way of thinking, a school of thought that will at long last help mankind do away with war and bloodshed.

However, there are so many quatrains referring to the terrors of a nuclear holocaust and a third world war that it's difficult to see how it could be avoided and a golden age of peace could possibly be ushered in. Or is it? Maybe Nostradamus is saying that either we can avoid total destruction by silencing the dogs of war or, failing that, maybe those left after the nuclear holocaust will come together to build a more perfect world. In several quatrains, Nostradamus offers us

Below: Some experts on Nostradamus feel that the coming cataclysm could take the form of a hugely destructive earthquake, far greater than the one that struck Los Angeles in the early 1990s.

Above: However, though some quatrains suggest that much will be destroyed, others can be interpreted as offering the promise of a golden age of peace and harmony.

the hope that we can and will survive, if we heed the warnings. He talks of a world at peace for thousands of years, even if this generation and the next does almost destroy civilization as we know it.

"Twenty-seven years after the reign of the moon passes,
Seven thousand years another will hold his monarchy.
When the sun takes up his final cycle,
Then is my prophecy accomplished and ended."

Century I Quatrain 48

He appears to be telling us that mankind will last 7,000 years after his own time, despite the terrors that might be fast approaching.

"Mars and Jupiter will be in conjunction,
A calamitous war under Cancer.
A short time afterward a new king will be anointed
Who will bring peace to the earth for a long time."

Century VI, Quatrain 24

Here, the prophet says that after the terrible war of Cancer – which he predicted earlier will occur through the evil doings of the third Antichrist in July, 1999 – a new 'king' will appear when Mars and Jupiter are in conjunction, something that happens every two years or so. This new 'king' – whether he be

Above: The image of birds in flight is used by Nostradamus to suggest new ideas, perhaps a great teacher, to enable people to transcend the awful fate predicted elsewhere in his writings.
Below: These 'rare birds' will be the harbingers of a new era of harmony and tranquillity, in which mankind will finally learn to live in harmony with the planet.

ORBITS OF THE PLANETS

THE EARTH

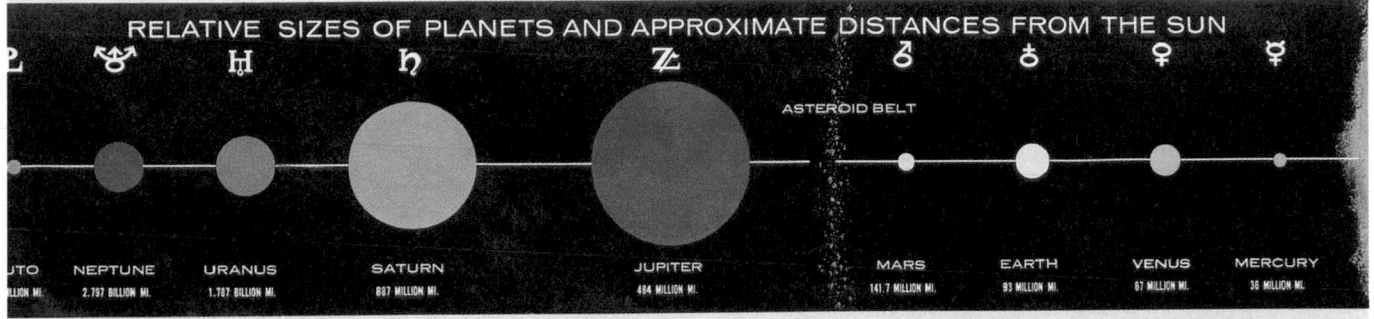

RELATIVE SIZES OF PLANETS AND APPROXIMATE DISTANCES FROM THE SUN

ASTEROID BELT

PLUTO	NEPTUNE	URANUS	SATURN	JUPITER	MARS	EARTH	VENUS	MERCURY
MILLION MI.	2.797 BILLION MI.	1.787 BILLION MI.	887 MILLION MI.	484 MILLION MI.	141.7 MILLION MI.	93 MILLION MI.	67 MILLION MI.	36 MILLION MI.

MOON

EARTH

VENUS

MERCURY

SUN

MARS

SOLAR PROMINENCE

SATURN

JUPITER

URANUS

THE SOLAR SYSTEM

Left: In the middle of the 20th century utopian thinkers saw the future as a cleaner, better version of their own day, in which better technology would eliminate human want and suffering.

Above: The planets of the solar system exercise subtle gravitational pulls on the earth. Usually they cancel one another out, but occasionally the planets line up to produce much stronger effects.

statesman, religious leader or visionary – will arrive into the world early in the next millennium. A short time after the war is over, this great man of peace will bring tranquillity to the world for 'a long time'.

> *"There will be peace, union and change,*
> *Estates and offices low, high; those high,*
> *very low.*
> *To prepare for a journey torments the first.*
> *War to cease, civil processes, debates."*

Century IX, Quatrain 66

In this quatrain of our future, Nostradamus seems to speak of a period following the madness of the great war

that lies just ahead. He clearly sees a period in which war is no more – where armed conflict is replaced by civilized debate – and a time of unity among the peoples of the Earth. The second line of the quatrain tells us that positions people today find important will later be insignificant, while those considered trifling now will one day become more meaningful. Is he predicting that in this golden new age we no longer place such importance on a person's wealth, or how many homes he or she owns, or what social background he or she comes from? The third line is quite interesting also. The latest thinking is that 'the first' refers to the youth of this new age, who

MARTIAN GENESIS

The idea of man someday venturing into space is not as far-fetched as one might think. Even today, NASA believes that Mars could one day be a recreational and agricultural adjunct to the Earth. Although the project is strictly theoretical at this stage, it is not pure science fiction. One day, scientists hope to transform Mars – or 'terraform' it – from a dead, frozen wasteland into a living, breathing planet. This will require a little help from pollution, bacteria and maybe a couple of hundred nuclear weapons.

Basically, the broad outline calls for warming Mars by about 100°F to unlock the frozen water on the polar caps and underground, and then recycling its atmosphere of carbon dioxide into oxygen. While the 'genesis' of Mars is still centuries away, the idea is on the drawing board.

According to the most likely scenario, Mars would be warmed by spraying millions of ton of chlorofluorocarbons into its atmosphere. These 'greenhouse' gases would trap heat on the Martian surface, and warm it to Earth-like temperatures in about 200 years, melting its polar caps and getting rivers to flow. The gases, scientists believe, could be manufactured on the planet in specially-sealed factories; several million tons could be released each year.

If the factory idea does not work, there have even been suggestions that man could nudge an asteroid out of its orbit and onto a collision course with Mars by using a few hundred nuclear warheads. The resulting impact would produce a crater hot enough to release trapped gases and water in the Martian landscape. Others prefer comets for this planetary excavation, because they wouldn't need a nuclear nudge and carry huge amounts of frozen water. A flurry of small explosions on the Oort clouds beyond Pluto would send a million comets onto

Many 20th-century artists have attempted to envision what a trip to Mars might look like, but Nostradamus foresaw life beyond the Earth 400 years ago.

Mars. The only problem with this would be the chance of missing Mars and hitting Earth. The last time that happened, the dinosaurs were done in!

Once the planet was sufficiently warmed and its water flowing, the next big step would be to produce oxygen from a poisonous carbon dioxide atmosphere. Here on Earth, microbes did the job some 3.5 billion years ago but, with a little innovative thinking, humans could produce breathable air on Mars within 15 years. Some scientists envision a series of "terrabubbles" – plastic domes that would safeguard the microbes from the outside atmosphere and allow them to generate an oxygen-rich environment. Eventually, higher forms of life, including man, could move in.

Other experts prefer the idea of transforming the entire planet. Mel Averner and Robert MacElroy, two NASA scientists who wrote the first study on terraforming in 1976, say vast mats of lichen and algae laid down like sod could begin producing oxygen. Left to their own devices, these microbes could take 100,000 years to do the job, so planetary microbiologists suggest using genetically-engineered microbes to produce more oxygen more efficiently. These 'designer bugs' should also be changed to resist radiation, and could eventually help produce a breathable atmosphere. Because the deadly ultraviolet radiation which constantly bombards the Martian surface would kill off the top layer, the 'mats' would have to be protected by a dusting of soil.

will undertake a great journey – whether a spiritual journey of renewal as we have already discussed, an actual journey such as the exploration of the solar system, or something else entirely, is open to interpretation. Support for all interpretations can be found in other quatrains and writings.

Beyond the Future

In another preface, Nostradamus wrote: "Before the moon has finished her entire cycle, the Sun and then Saturn will come. According to the Celestial signs, the reign of Saturn will come a second time, so that all is calculated, the world draws near to is final death dealing cycle." This is a powerful prediction, offering a degree of hope for those generations who

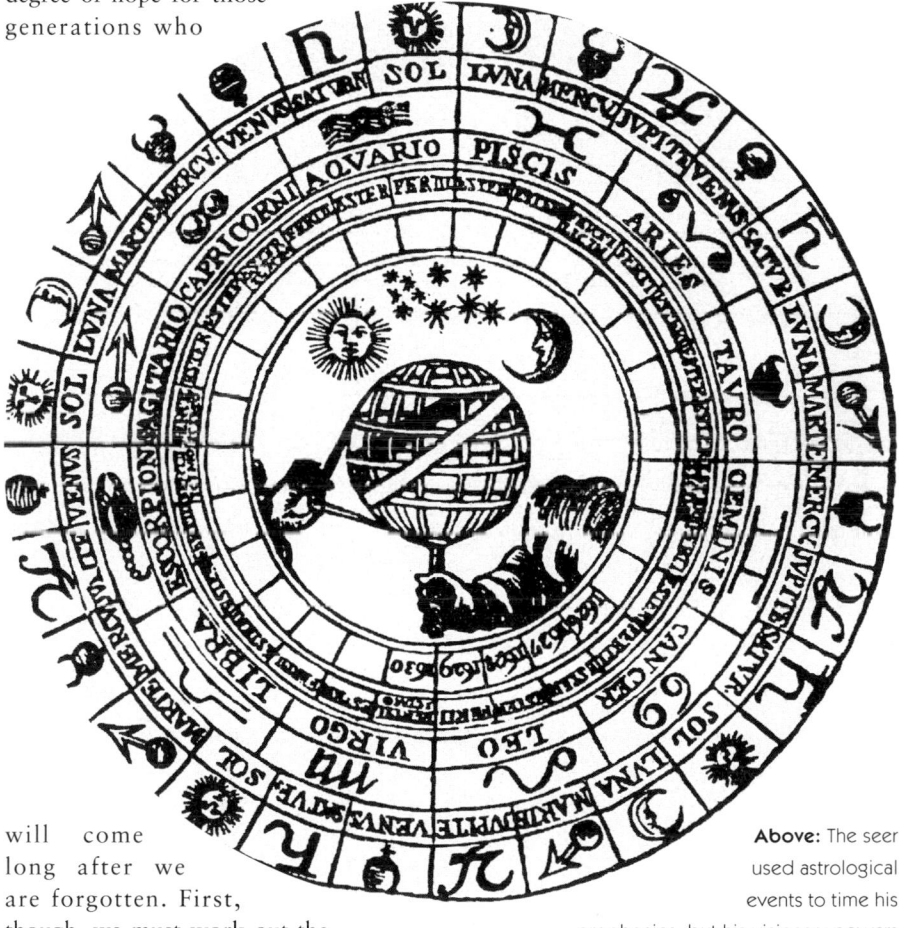

will come long after we are forgotten. First, though, we must work out the dates in the passage. The moon will finish her cycle in 2250, then will come the reign of Saturn – the Age of Aquarius – followed by a second coming of Saturn, this time the Age of Capricorn. In the astrology of Nostradamus's day, Saturn ruled both Aquarius and Capricorn. The prophet appears to be telling us that during the age of

Capricorn (between 4000 and 6000 AD), the world draws near to its end, probably as the result of some cosmic cataclysm. Interestingly, Nostradamus once wrote in a letter to his son, César, that the world would end in 3979.

Where is the hope in all of this? Before we discuss that, let us first take a look at how Nostradamus believes the world will finally come to an end.

"A very mighty quake in the month of May, Saturn in Capricorn. Jupiter and Mercury in Taurus.
Venus also in Cancer, Mars in Virgo.
Hail will fall greater than an egg."

Century 10, Quatrain 67

Above: The seer used astrological events to time his prophecies, but his visionary powers were not dependent on reading horoscopes.

This uncommon astrological alignment will next occur in the year 3755 – a little over 40 years before Nostradamus' predicted end of the world. A mighty earthquake, the likes of which has never been seen before in history, will strike in the month of May,

Above: Nostradamus wrote to his elder son, César, telling him he foresaw that the world would end when floodwaters obliterated most of the land. Could this mean that the polar ice-caps will melt?

likely the result of some cosmic occurrence which will tear the earth's crust apart. In a frightening preface to César, he sees "Before the universal conflagration the world will be deluged by many floods to such heights that there will remain scarcely any land not covered by water, and this will last for so long that everything will perish except the truth itself and the races which inhabit it. Furthermore, before and after these floods, many nations shall see no rains and there will fall from the sky such a great amount of fire and meteors that nothing will remain unconsumed. All this will happen a short time before the final conflagration."

Leaving the planet
So if the world is going to end in the year 3797AD, where is the hope for mankind that Nostradamus is predicting? Remember, the prophet envisions the end of the world – not of mankind. The answer, it seems, lies in the stars. By the time of the great upheavals that will consign the Earth to destruction, Nostradamus predicts we will have conquered space, and set up colonies on distant planets.

In one of his epistles, he wrote that "The world will be approaching a great conflagration, although, according to my calculations in my prophecies, the course of time runs much further." The 'course of time' is, presumably, human time, meaning that some future generations will escape the catastrophe and return to the heavens whence we originally came and live among the stars.

Is this the 'great revelation' Nostradamus predicted would come to pass more than 400 years ago?

"For five hundred years more they will take notice of him.
Who was the ornament of his time.
Then suddenly a great revelation will be made
Which will make the people of that century well pleased."

Century III Quatrain 94

Nostradamus might be telling us here that five hundred years after his *Centuries* were published – which is less than 60 years away – someone will interpret one of his quatrains and provide untold benefit for mankind. Is there lurking somewhere in the many unsolved quatrains the answer which will give us the keys to the universe? It could well be, but according to Nostradamus, it's an impossible question for those of our generation to answer – after all, the interpretation is still some six decades away.

Extraordinary gift
It is on this quizzical note that we come to the end of our journey through time with the prophet of Salon, who was blessed with the extraordinary gift of seeing tomorrow in all its horror and hope. In the years since he published the first of his *Centuries*, he has continued to beguile, amaze and frighten us. He told us of things that we who are alive today can now call history, and of things yet to come, but most of all, he has beckoned us from across the centuries to re-evaluate our beliefs, our lifestyles and our actions. Dare we not follow him?

Above and Left: It is a tribute to the breadth of Nostradamus's vision that a country doctor who never travelled more than a few hundred miles from his birthplace saw the day when humanity would leave the planet that cradled it to seek its ultimate destiny in the stars.

Index